YOU'RE A CELEBRITY,
GET YOURSELF OUT THERE!

YOU'RE A CELEBRITY, GET YOURSELF OUT THERE!

An unconventional guide to
leveraging fame, celebrity and PR to
take you from influential to iconic

BRENDA GABRIEL

authors
AND CO.

First published in Great Britain in 2024
by Authors & Co.
www.authorsandco.pub

ISBN 978-1-915771-93-3 (paperback)

CONTENTS

FOREWORD

This book is for the disruptors, the pioneers, and those who dare to dream big. It's for you, the sometimes unseen hero who, day in and day out, is transforming lives without fanfare.

My mission, through these pages, is to give you the confidence to take up space and make yourself seen—not for the sake of fame or becoming a celebrity but for the sake of making the difference only you can make in the world.

I believe we need more everyday heroes in our newspapers, on our TV screens, and in the public eye. This belief is what sparked my desire to get into PR once I realised the power of mass media.

I don't know about you, but I want to hear more about the kind of people whose message or work is quietly making a difference, but who rarely get the recognition they deserve. It's time to change that. I want to see these unsung heroes—like you—celebrated with the same energy and admiration we give A-list celebrities because the truth is, your influence is just as valuable—if not more.

The tragic passing of Caroline Flack in 2020 was a turning point for me. It wasn't just another news story—it was a painful reminder of the relentless pressures that come with visibility and how even the most experienced, media-savvy public figures can find themselves on the receiving end of overwhelming public scrutiny, which can take a huge toll.

Caroline lived just minutes away from me. The proximity of her death hit hard.

While the media furore sensationalised every aspect of her life and social media exploded with vitriol, Caroline was advised against sharing her truth.

I wondered and still do, whether having her voice heard could have possibly changed things.

My frustration with the media's role in amplifying the highs and lows of public life without considering the emotional toll was compounded by the fact that, for years, I've worked with entrepreneurs, thought leaders, and visionaries, helping them prepare for life in the spotlight. I've seen firsthand how exposure affects them—not just professionally, but personally. Fame and fortune are two sides of the same coin, but without emotional resilience, that coin can become a burden.

On the other side of this, there are countless people who don't know that the support they need exists—because the individuals who could help aren't prominent enough to be known by the very people who need their work the most.

This book isn't just about PR strategies or media appearances—it's about building a presence that's rooted in authenticity and integrity. It's about helping you, the disruptor, the dreamer, the quiet hero, to step into the light and be celebrated for the work you're doing. It's about giving you the tools to navigate the world of visibility while staying grounded in who you are and the impact you want to create.

I've struggled with my own fears of being seen, of putting myself out there. But staying hidden doesn't serve anyone. I want to empower you to step into your own spotlight and use your influence for good. It's not always an easy journey, but it's one worth taking.

This book is my way of sharing everything I've learned about navigating visibility, influence, and the media so that more heroes like you can rise up and make the impact the world so desperately needs.

To your ascendancy.

Brenda Gabriel
Self-Proclaimed Fame PR Queen

SETTING THE STAGE

"When you realise fame is a tool and not the end goal, you no longer fear being seen as a celebrity"

– Brenda Gabriel

What comes up for you when you hear the word 'celebrity'? Maybe it makes you want to roll your eyes at the inane headlines and vacuous stories in the media you're subjected to about people you couldn't care less about. Perhaps it's the glitz and glamour of ostentatiously dressed A-Listers on the red carpet and flashing cameras. Maybe the constant scrutiny and invasion of privacy that comes with being in the public eye. You might even think of influencers with millions of followers who seem to have it all but are often just as flawed and human as the rest of us. Whatever it is, celebrity is a word that triggers strong reactions, whether envy, admiration, scepticism or even disdain. Here's the thing: what if you had the power to change the meaning of what it means to be a celebrity? What if it didn't have to be about fame for fame's sake? What if you could be part of a movement to make it about something greater than who's wearing what or dating who?

That's what this book aims to do. To me, celebrity is less about designer clothes and more about the power of influence, the ability to shape opinions, inspire action and, when used wisely, drive real change.

When I first started my PR agency, I talked a lot about fame for entrepreneurs. I was often told that entrepreneurs have no interest in being famous. They do what they do for impact, not notoriety.

I've encountered many brilliant minds dedicated to making a significant impact in their fields. A great number are reluctant to be perceived as an influencer or, even worse, a celebrity.

Accidental fame? Sure!

Purposeful fame? No thanks!

What if fame wasn't a shallow, narcissistic pursuit but a powerful ally in crafting your legacy? What if it was the difference between impacting millions and your unrealised potential being buried or cremated with you? What if it was about amplifying your world-shifting ideas that you could live to see realised?

For me, fame magnifies our ability to influence, lead and inspire action on a grand scale.

It makes you a beacon for those who share your values and aspirations. It magnetises attention, resources, partnerships and opportunities that can scale impact far beyond what any individual effort can achieve.

Imagine your ideas, framework or modality being responsible for transforming your industry. Imagine your work becoming a catalyst for social change.

How would it feel to be remembered as a cultural agent whose philosophies will be immortalised not just as part of this zeitgeist but an instigator of it, contributing to the next stage of societal evolution or advancement?

Does that feel vacuous?

My desire for you to embrace fame is not for the accolades or recognition but for the doors it opens. Not just for you but for those coming after you, the causes you champion and the changes you wish to see in the world.

I say we redefine fame.

We see it as any other tool: a means to an end. A way of ensuring your innovations, ideas and values leave a lasting imprint on the world. Your legacy deserves to be known and celebrated. When we shift our perspective on fame, we unlock the potential to create a legacy that transcends our own lifetime.

Celebrity can be a tool, a platform and, yes, even a responsibility, but that's what makes it so valuable. My hope is that by the end of this book, when you think of fame and celebrity, you won't just picture glossy magazine covers; you will think of the potential it holds for you to make an impact, to be a force for good in your industry and beyond.

Of course, being a celebrity is not essential to having a successful business or career, nor is it essential to making a difference in the lives of others through your work. Though what I will say is that in my many years of experience as a publicist, I've seen time and time again that those with the biggest profiles have the biggest influence and, as such, the biggest potential for mass impact.

Anyone who has a desire to touch the lives of those beyond their current sphere will need to be known by the right people to make that a reality.

The fastest most effective method to do this at scale is public relations (PR). When done effectively, PR will help you go from unknown to an icon. With the advent of social media and now AI, there's never been a better time to leverage the media to reach global audiences with your unique insights, being the change you wish to see in the world and craft a lasting legacy.

In this book, we'll explore how you can redefine 'celebrity' on your terms, using it as a force for good. We will delve into the strategies and mindset that can help you navigate the world of PR, media and public perception, so you can stand out not just for what you do but for the impact you make.

Whether you're an entrepreneur, a thought leader or someone with a burning passion to change the world, I invite you to take this journey with me. Let's rethink what it means to be a celebrity, and use that power to make a difference.

WHO IS THIS BOOK FOR?

If you're expecting a standard DIY PR manual with basic guidelines on how to pitch the media to get yourself onto *Good Morning Britain/America*, secure a *Forbes* feature or get into *Cosmopolitan* magazine, you might want to stop reading here. There are enough DIY PR books on the market giving advice on how to do all of the above. Adding to the cacophony of what's already been said many times before seems like a wasted opportunity. Instead, I'd like to take you a level deeper and share my personal insights and experience on how taking a holistic, strategic approach rather than tactical to PR and relationship building will help you get far better outcomes in less time, not just in business but in life.

So you've picked up this book and are wondering, "Is this for me?" Maybe you're an entrepreneur who's tired of being the best-kept secret of your industry, an executive who's ready to step out from behind the corporate curtain and build your own personal brand, a music artist ready to blow up or an influencer who's ready to do more than skits on TikTok. If you've ever dreamed of being recognised for your brilliance, of having people know who you are and what you stand for, then yes, this book is absolutely for you!

Let's break it down, shall we?

THE VISIONARY

You have a clear vision of how your unique insights and expertise could change the world if you could get reach enough people. You're not just content with thinking outside the box; you don't even see the box. If you're ready to share your genius with the world, but maybe aren't sure how to grow your following and get more people to sit up and pay attention. This is where PR comes in. You're out there making things happen but understand the importance of working smarter, not harder.

THE EXECUTIVE

You've climbed the corporate ladder, navigated the politics and now you're sitting pretty at the top, or perhaps a few rungs away. You have the title, the corner office, the power… You may have plans to leave corporate or set up your own side hustle. Perhaps you already have the side hustle set up and would like to make a bigger name for yourself. You want to influence, inspire and fulfil your potential. If you're ready to transition from being the best-kept secret in your organisation to the go-to expert everyone wants to hear from, this is for you.

THE LEADING EXPERT

You're incredibly successful in real world terms and are wondering what's next. You have already attained the level of success and revenue most could only dream of. You have worked with major global brands and have a CV that reads like a who's who of business. You have worked long and hard to get to where you are and are well respected in certain influential circles. You are likely to have created or begun to create your own modality and know that getting it the hands of the right people has the potential to disrupt your industry and affect social change, impacting millions.

You have hit the pinnacle of your industry in many ways, but your name is synonymous with where you've been, not where you're going. Your business is currently successful, but the direction you see it heading in requires you to stay not just in your zone of genius but in your zone of excellence. You are making money and getting clients but you desire more. Your level of expertise far excels that of your peers and those with celebrity status in your field, but you aren't attracting the same level of opportunities or commanding the same rates as them because in this day and age audience size and notoriety rule.

The work you do needs specific exposure to reach the right people. Your ideal clients aren't to be found hanging out online in FB groups; they're more likely to be on a golf course or at a charity event. Your longevity and success in business speaks for itself, but your search results and online presence belie your peerless capabilities.

You know there must be an easier way to get the recognition you deserve but aren't quite sure what.

Uncover how PR and media exposure holds the key to your resurgence, leveraging your previous success and pivoting your personal brand whilst increasing your status and revenue.

THE CREATIVE

You're the artist, the musician, the writer, the designer. You live and breathe creativity. But sometimes it feels like you're screaming into the void and the void isn't exactly shouting back. You have the talent but you need the world to see it. This book is for you because you're ready to stop being a starving artist and start being a celebrated one. Let's get your name in lights!

THE INFLUENCER

You have the followers, the likes and the aesthetic feed that would make a Kardashian jealous. You're not just here for the double taps; you want to make an impact. You're ready to be known for more than just #OOTD posts. This book is for you because you're serious about building a brand that lasts, one that's more than just a flash in the social media pan.

THE FEARFUL DREAMER

Now, let's talk about the elephant in the room: fear. Maybe you're reading this thinking, "Sure, I want to be known, but what if I'm not ready? What if I mess up? What if I become too famous and can't even go to the grocery store without being mobbed?" Hold up! This book is most definitely for you because guess what? Everyone has those fears. The difference is that the people who make it big learn to manage that fear and channel it into something productive. You don't have to be fearless to be famous; your why just needs to be bigger than your fear.

THE IMPACT SEEKER

Finally, this book is for those of you who want to do more than just make a name for yourself; you want to make a difference. You're not just in this for fame and fortune (although, let's be honest, those are nice perks); you want to use your platform to create real, lasting change. Whether it's advocating for a cause, inspiring a movement or just making the world a little brighter, this book is for you because you're ready to harness the power of PR for good.

Whichever of these categories you fall into, you must be willing to leave behind the comfort of being one of many and take up the mantle as an industry icon and agent of change.

The planning and execution of a PR and publicity strategy bespoke to you, is the fastest, most effective way to work towards this.

You're ready to get the recognition, rates and opportunities you deserve and you know that getting noticed is half the battle.

If any of these descriptions resonate with you, then welcome aboard! This book is your roadmap to not just getting noticed but making an impact. It's time to stop talking about the impact you'd love to make and get out there to make it. Are you ready for your renaissance?

Let's go!

A CONFESSION

Before we get stuck in, I want to make a confession of sorts. Although this is a PR book, the purpose of writing this is not to teach you how to go and DIY yourself to fame. If you decide you want to, that's on you, but I'm a strong believer in experts staying in their zone of genius. The biggest waste of time as a business owner or CEO is dropping your genius work to do something that can be outsourced, and not to anyone, but to someone who can do a far better job than you can. One of the first things I outsourced once my business took off was a cleaner. Can I clean? Yes. Do I enjoy it? Sometimes. Can I do a faster, more efficient job than a professional cleaner? Not a chance. Do I generate more in my business per hour than the £20 it costs to outsource the cleaning? Yes. That is why I outsource my cleaning despite the fact I'm more than capable of doing my own. I feel the same way about outsourcing PR.

Those who know me know I make no secret of the fact that I'm not a fan of DIY shoestring PR past a certain point or business. I have seen first-hand the negative impact when PR goes wrong and the resulting fallout. Building and managing a reputation is challenging enough for a communications specialist, let alone as a business owner with competing business priorities, so this book will not provide you with an end-to-end process of how to become your own publicist.

However, as a publicist often approached by disgruntled founders and experts several thousand pounds lighter because of investing with the wrong PR agency, and as a business owner who has invested in services that didn't offer the support I didn't realise I required until it was too late, I'm also not a fan of people paying for a service they don't fully understand.

Four of my biggest PR industry bugbears (and the catalyst behind writing this book) are:

1. LACK OF UNDERSTANDING OF PR AND ITS BENEFITS

For as long as I've been in PR, it's been apparent hardly anyone outside the industry understands what PR is and what its tangible benefits are. As a result, many avoid implementing a PR strategy altogether, thinking that it can be interchanged with clever social media marketing, ads or hiring and focusing solely on sales activity. As a result, many end up working much harder than they need to on building a pipeline, scaling their business, getting recognition, building their audience, securing promotions, paid speaking opportunities or investment etc.

Many invest in PR believing that hiring an agency will lead to instant fame or the guarantee of going viral, a dramatic increase in rates and those willing to pay them, an avalanche of clients and a reality TV show, all with minimal input from themselves.

Whilst it's true that PR done in the right way can help achieve these results, as seen with many of my PR clients, this is only half the story.

Media relations and publicity (earned media coverage) on TV and in mainstream publications will obviously help increase visibility by exposing you to a wider audience. Being endorsed by brands that are well established, perceived as high in authority and also held in high regard helps with positioning you as a more credible and trustworthy prospect to your audience, allowing you to be perceived as the go-to in your industry.

Other benefits include raising brand awareness, and such lesser talked-about benefits such as enhancing brand equity, forging long-term, valuable relationships and gaining 'top of mindshare'.

What on earth is mindshare?

Think of a popular fizzy drink…

Did you think of Coca-Cola?

If you did, that's mindshare at work and confirmation that Coca-Cola's strategic marketing, advertising and integrated PR strategy have effectively placed their beverage as top of mind when their audience thinks of a fizzy drink. You may not even like Coca-Cola, but the company's consistent, strategic PR efforts have been so effective that brand awareness has increased to the point of becoming ingrained in the public consciousness, making it synonymous with the entire category of carbonated beverages. This kind of top-of-mind awareness doesn't happen overnight; it comes as the result of a sustained and well-executed PR strategy over a long period of time.

When people think of the benefits of PR, they are invariably concerned about going 'viral' and ot a financial return on investment (ROI). Rather than focusing on one viral post or meme – because consistently going viral isn't possible – PR focuses on delivering sustainable visibility and engagement. Whilst increased brand awareness will almost certainly lead to an increase in sales over time, the main benefit of investing in PR is *not* directly monetary.

The true value of PR lies in its ability to help build authentic relationships and a recognisable, trusted brand that resonates with your audience. A trusted brand is a brand with longevity. A positive perception and experience of a brand encourages loyalty, something that is invaluable in today's market.

Over time, these relationships can, and often do, lead to new partnerships, collaborations and growth.

Just as with any solid relationship, this takes time. Contrary to what you may have been led to believe with celebrations of major features or a TV interview, PR is not a one-and-done job.

PR is a long game.

2. LACK OF TRANSPARENCY IN THE PR PROCESS

Those who have a basic understanding of PR but not what the benefits specifically for them could be, either invest in DIY PR solutions that offer little to no insight into the strategy (rather than one-off tactics) required to achieve impactful results over time, or they hire PR firms without a understanding the PR process, level of input required from them and what outcomes are realistic within the given timescales and budget.

Often, ineffective strategies are sold based on the budget of a client rather than what that client actually needs, leaving clients feeling out of the loop and disillusioned, leading to frustration and a sense of having wasted money when the unrealistic anticipated levels of recognition and likely sales are not achieved.

3. PR HAS THE WORST PR

Possibly outside of the existence of the job of an actuary (I only discovered this job existed in the past few years), I honestly believe the job of a publicist is probably one of the least understood and most underrated, so much so it sometimes appears every Jane, Jo and Daisy from non-PR backgrounds believe they can do it. The number of online business coaches, marketers and even sales coaches who advertise DIY PR as an add on, under the guise of increasing visibility or profile-raising as a direct ticket to increasing sales or attracting more clients, has grown over the past few years. Whilst I respect the hustle, and some indeed may be well placed to offer their insights to those not in a position to pay thousands of pounds a month to an agency, there are many more who are not.

What I personally find sad about this is that many smaller online-based PR agencies and freelance publicists often find themselves competing on price with non-experts (and, increasingly, AI software solutions) for clients, as it can be difficult to articulate the value of experience, creativity and strategic thinking required to execute an integrated PR campaign week after week, month after month, year after year.

Prospects often have little to no idea the level of skill required to deliver consistent results on a campaign or the number moving parts when it comes to building, maintaining and then protecting a brand and its reputation. That's before we even begin to think about crisis management.

Don't get me wrong, PR isn't rocket science. Almost anyone with training or media contacts can craft a pitch, give an interview or write an article. Most could secure a few earned pieces of coverage, though few have the creativity, energy or inclination to continue to come up with new angles or ways to maintain sustained media interest and public engagement over a sustained period of time.

PR is more than being able to write a press release or successfully pitch a national newspaper; it involves being able to take a seemingly unrelated angle, topic or event and making it relevant to the brand, the journalist, the outlet and the audience and the ability to foresee and navigate not just potential opportunities but pitfalls. The most effective PR involves constant monitoring, quick thinking and a strategic mindset to turn even the smallest opportunities into significant wins.

It's about recognising the best time to share a message for maximum impact and forging relationships with journalists, influencers, the public, as well as other stakeholders, ensuring the brand continues to be perceived as relevant and respected.

Crisis planning and management require an almost entirely different set of skills, a cool head for one, an ability to proactively mitigate damage ahead of time, address negative press or feedback head on and work to maintain public trust in a brand.

4. LACK OF SUPPORT FOR ENTREPRENEURS ENTERING THE PUBLIC EYE

Something I don't hear talked about but feel very passionate about is the lack of support available to regular people who find themselves thrust into the spotlight.

I have yet to encounter an entrepreneur who started their business with the purpose of being famous. In my experience, those who do attain fame often do so by chance.

Having worked in PR for over 10 years, I can say from experience that many entrepreneurs who experience some level of fame as a result of publicity, aren't prepared for the level of scrutiny, pressure and expectation that comes with handling new levels of exposure, public attention and perceived success. Whilst they may be industry experts, navigating the complexities of media interactions, public perception and maintaining authenticity under the public gaze can be daunting without proper guidance.

Standard and DIY PR offerings fail to provide the necessary support, leaving emerging public figures unprepared for the challenges that come with increased visibility.

People who find themselves going viral or being trolled, are vulnerable to emotional stress and to making missteps that could damage their brand or reputation. They may struggle with handling criticism or maintaining boundaries in a way that doesn't compromise their professional image. The emotional toll of being in the public eye can be significant.

The need for mentorship and ongoing support as one's profile grows is critical not just for managing the mechanics of public relations but empowering individuals to confidently embrace their new public roles.

Whilst this involves coaching on media skills, personal branding and crisis management, it also requires mental and emotional support to help them navigate the challenges of visibility.

This starts with understanding the importance of inside-out worthiness, authority and visibility. I truly believe if you don't feel worthy, authoritative, or truly want to be seen, no amount of PR activity will get you to your next level.

It's unbelievable the number of people say they don't want fame but are holding out to go viral; not realising the cognitive dissonance they operate from. When it comes to stepping into the spotlight it's important to make sure both our conscious and subconscious is onboard lest we find ourselves sabotaging our success to ensure we keep playing small.

As we move forward, we'll explore the profound impact that positioning yourself as an industry celebrity can have on your personal brand and the trajectory of your career. In the next chapter, we'll dive into the essence of fame and celebrity and why they are not just desirable goals but potent tools for shaping the world around you.

We will also delve into why I do PR the way I do. From my boutique approach to providing high-touch, personalised services to ensuring clients are prepared both operationally and emotionally, my methods are designed to help you attain greater levels of fame while living on purpose.

By the end of this book, you'll see fame, celebrity and the media as powerful tools for achieving your goals and creating a lasting legacy. You will understand that PR is not just about securing coverage; it is about building relationships, leveraging opportunities and positioning yourself as a thought leader and change-maker.

I'm not sure how well what's in my head will translate into what I intend for you to take from this book.

The irony of such a statement coming from a communications expert is not lost on me; neither is the fact that at the heart of public relations are the requirements to:

- Master the skill of bridging the gap between the denotation and connotation of a message.
- Spark and nurture relationships.
- Build and manage reputation.

This book is my attempt to do B with you and equip you with the tools to do all three for yourself.

I am trusting that the message you are meant to receive is the one that you do.

Embrace the journey and leverage the media to become a conscious celebrity, let's embark on this journey together, starting with an understanding of why I believe that you were born to be famous, in the way that feels good to you.

Enjoy!

INTRODUCTION

FROM THE SHADOWS TO THE SPOTLIGHT – MY MOTIVATION

If you'd told me fifteen years ago I'd be writing a PR book, calling myself a PR expert, I'd have laughed and asked for some of what you were on. Being completely transparent, I've had my own battles with fear and anxiety about stepping into the spotlight.

That annoying little voice demanding, "Who are you to call yourself an expert?" every time I step outside my comfort zone. A similar voice to the one many women tell me holds them back from going all in on their BIG vision. For a long time, I let that voice win.

One day, something shifted. It wasn't an overnight transformation nor a sudden burst of confidence. It was triggered by the tragic death of TV presenter Caroline Flack in 2020. Caroline, who lived a five-minute walk away from me at the time, had tragically taken her own life. Caroline was loved by many but was deeply troubled. Towards the end of her life, her entire life was being played out in the media like some twisted reality freak show, not just in the tabloids and TV but on social media. It was horrific to witness.

A TRAGIC WAKE-UP CALL: THE DEATH OF CAROLINE FLACK

Caroline was one of a long line of women in the public eye, scrutinised and hounded by the press during a time of personal crisis to the extent where they reached breaking point. It was painful to see the backpedaling of the media, deleting scathing articles online to replace them with calls for kindness, echoing one of Caroline's final Instagram posts posted two months before her passing: "In a world when you can be anything, be kind."

This hit close to home not just because of our geographical proximity, but because it was a stark reminder of the devastating impact that relentless public scrutiny can have on someone's mental health and the urgent need for a more compassionate approach to how we treat public figures, especially in times of personal crisis.

As someone who works in PR, I couldn't help but think about the role that responsible media coverage, supportive public relations and the right professional support could have played in her life. If only there had been a professional or network of professionals around her who could have helped her navigate the intense pressures she was facing. Perhaps things could have been different.

It felt like the media and authorities both failed to grasp the modern-day pervasiveness of online media, how it amplified the challenges of being famous and its damaging effects on the mental health of public figures. Having worked in the online space, I had seen not only how celebrities struggled with intense interest in their private lives, but also how entrepreneurs and business owners reacted to the emotional toll of being trolled, going viral, or landing several national press features. With increased exposure, the emotional strain was clear, often leading to self-sabotage.

I had learned both through my work and personally being trolled how judgement and condemnation from strangers could mess with your head. In 2017 I was trolled for sharing the story of my miscarriage with the tabloid press. It was then I realised that building emotional stability was crucial for anyone thrust into the limelight, be it celebrities, entrepreneurs, or public figures.

It was clear to me then, and even more so now, that navigating fame requires just as much emotional resilience as business acumen. Recognising the familiar feeling of internal contraction, discomfort and anxiety I felt when growing my business to 6-figures as someone who grew up on government assistance, I understood that fame and fortune were two sides of the same coin.

I began championing the idea in my content. From that time I've have been committed to ensuring that the work I do goes beyond just building fame; it also focuses on providing emotional support through mentorship of PR clients who are emerging into the spotlight. I didn't know back then that my aim would be to do my part to create a world where kindness, understanding, mental health and the emotional stability of someone putting themselves on the front line was prioritised just as much as headlines, public appearances and making money.

I wanted to put humanity at the front and centre of PR.

Caroline's death was a harsh reminder of the dark side of fame: the relentless scrutiny, the judgement and pressure that often comes with being in the public eye. Despite her success and fame, Caroline was struggling. She wanted to be heard not as Caroline the celebrity, but as Carrie the woman. After her passing, Caroline's family released a post she had written and wanted to share to explain her side of the story.

Here it is in full:

> *"For a lot of people, being arrested for common assault is an extreme way to have some sort of spiritual awakening but for me it's become the normal.*
> *I've been pressing the snooze button on many stresses in my life - for my whole life. I've accepted shame and toxic opinions on my life for over 10 years and yet told myself it's all part of my job. No complaining.*
> *The problem with brushing things under the carpet is they are still there and one day someone is going to lift that carpet up and all you are going to feel is shame and embarrassment.*
> *On December the 12th 2019 I was arrested for common assault on my boyfriend. Within 24 hours my whole world and future was swept from under my feet and all the walls that I had taken so long to build around me collapsed. I am suddenly on a different kind of stage and everyone is watching it happen.*
> *I have always taken responsibility for what happened that night. Even on the night. But the truth is... It was an accident.*
> *I've been having some sort of emotional breakdown for a very long time.*
> *But I am NOT a domestic abuser. We had an argument and an accident happened. An accident. The blood that*

> *someone SOLD to a newspaper was MY blood and that was something very sad and very personal.*
> *The reason I am talking today is because my family can't take anymore. I've lost my job. My home. My ability to speak. And the truth has been taken out of my hands and used as entertainment.*
> *I can't spend every day hidden away being told not to say or speak to anyone.*
> *I'm so sorry to my family for what I have brought upon them and for what my friends have had to go through.*
> *I'm not thinking about 'how I'm going to get my career back.' I'm thinking about how I'm going to get mine and my family's life back."*

Sadly, Caroline was reportedly advised by her team against sharing her true voice, her vulnerability, her pain. She was silenced, and not long after, she was gone.

As someone whose main facet of work involves encouraging people to share their truth, I was devastated that had been taken away from a woman who spoke publicly for a living at a time when she needed to be heard the most. I suspect it had something to do with the legal ramifications of swaying public opinion, but to me it seemed so unfair.

I couldn't shake the thought: What if I had been more visible? What if she had known I existed? What if I could have connected her with people who could have helped? This wasn't about me. At the time, I was working with a client involved in a project working on an AI-powered solution for patients flagged as high risk of self-harm.

I looked at my social media friends list and saw numerous talented individuals who had created their own modalities that had literally transformed the lives of clients, bringing them back from the brink of despair. There were others creating miracles for others every day. Whether helping people with health issues, fertility challenges, business growth, emotional freedom or overcoming trauma, I knew people out who could hugely benefit by having access to what these people have to offer. But if these experts remained hidden, how would the people who need them ever find them?

That's when it hit me: staying in the shadows isn't just a disservice to ourselves; it is a disservice to the people we can help.

My intention is not to simplify tragic circumstances or claim that any one person or solution would have prevented the outcome; it's about recognising that feeling seen, feeling understood, connection and the right support at the right time can make a difference.

It is about understanding that for every person struggling, both in and out of the limelight, there may be a solution out there – an expert, a modality or some other form of support that could help them – but not if they don't know it exists. That's why I believe so strongly in the power of mass visibility, to ensure the right people can be found by those who need them most.

Staying hidden, not stepping up to share what we can do for the world and playing small is more than a missed opportunity for us as professionals; it could mean the difference between someone finding the help they need or feeling alone and out of options. This realisation has fuelled my desire and commitment to helping others step into their light, share their truth and be seen, because being visible isn't about self-promotion; it is about service.

THE MISSING PIECE: MY VOICE

I was proud of what I had already achieved in my career. I'd landed coverage in high-profile publications and even helped numerous women increase their income, giving them more options in life. Yet, I felt something was missing. *I* was.

I was missing from the PR landscape as a pioneer of a new kind of PR, one that goes beyond the surface level of fame and celebrity and addresses the emotional and mental challenges that come with being in the public eye. I realised that the work that truly lights me up wasn't just about getting clients in the media; it was about helping them develop the emotional stamina needed for life in the spotlight.

Caroline's death was the catalyst that pushed me to step up and fully commit to this work. I had always refrained from offering DIY PR because I knew it wasn't enough. It is why a mentorship element was included in my bespoke PR work as standard. It is why I always emphasised the importance of both operational and emotional preparation for PR.

The problem? I didn't feel qualified to tell these clients who were so much more successful than me that their decision not to take my advice, take the opportunity, react to trolls or listen to bad advice from others was a form of self-sabotage to keep them playing small.

Not anymore.

I have dedicated the past four years to developing a methodology that goes beneath the surface layer of fame and celebrity as a commodity and turns both into vehicles for positive change. A key part of this work is the activation and sharing of a public figure's true voice and message.

In the industry, many people trade who they are for who they believe they need to be. Caroline was no different. As prepared as she was for professional knockbacks, she wasn't prepared for sharing her perceived failings or vulnerability with the entire world. At her most vulnerable, she wanted to be heard. But she was silenced, told her voice didn't matter.

This is why I'm so passionate about the work I do. I am here to make sure that every woman who works with me is heard, that people sit up and take notice when she speaks. This goes way beyond appearing in a few pieces of coverage; it is about challenging and changing the status quo, where women are not just seen but truly heard.

FROM THE CPS TO PR: BRIDGING THE GAP BETWEEN LAW AND MEDIA

Before I found my calling in PR, I worked in the Crown Prosecution Service (CPS). My background in the legal system gave me a unique perspective on the power of the media and public opinion. I saw firsthand how the narrative in the media could influence public perception and even legal outcomes.

I understood one of the reasons they may have decided to prosecute Caroline could have been related to the pressure of not being seen to be giving preferential treatment to a woman and celebrity in a case of domestic violence, without realising that being a woman in the public eye and the pervasiveness of social media does indeed add another aspect for consideration. Again, I wasn't in a position to lend my voice to the conversation as no one knew who I was.

If my PR methodology had been solidified earlier, could I have taken on an advisory role for celebrity cases, helping to navigate the tricky waters of public scrutiny and media pressure? Who knows?

This has fuelled my belief in the power of PR not just as a tool for publicity, but as a means of protecting and empowering those in the public eye. I am driven by the conviction that PR should be about more than just managing a brand's image; it should be about supporting the individuals behind the brand, ensuring they have the emotional and mental resilience to withstand the pressures of fame.

STEPPING UP FOR THOSE WHO COME AFTER

A month after her death, Caroline Flack came to me in a dream. It was vivid. She told me I needed to "step up for those coming up after her."

I used to be scared of talking about my brand of PR because it felt too 'out there', but now I see that this work is more important than ever. The world doesn't need more cookie-cutter PR strategies; it needs PR that's rooted in empathy, authenticity and a deep understanding of the human experience.

So here I am, stepping up, sharing my voice and writing this book not just for me but for all the people out there who need to be heard, who have something valuable to say but don't yet know how to say it in a way that resonates. This book is for those ready to step into the spotlight and make a difference.

In the end, it's not just about being visible; It's is about using your platform to shine a light on what truly matters and being a force for good in the world.

THE POWER OF BEING KNOWN

A while back, I was invited to a private event at Tramp, a legendary London nightclub, for a party with the boy band East 17. Champagne flowing, canapés everywhere and a guest list that read like a who's who of the celeb world. The most impactful aspect of the night? Not hanging out with celebs but the real, unfiltered conversations I had.

I spoke to a celeb journalist who shared her thoughts on the Colleen Rooney and Rebecca Vardy saga: a case study in how PR can either make or break you. A reality TV star who confided in me said she nearly didn't come because of a wardrobe malfunction earlier in the day, the fear of being snapped by the paparazzi in less-than-perfect attire causing major anxiety. Another reality star opened up about the anxiety they'd suffered since being thrust into the spotlight. Someone else confided that their recent birthday was less than celebratory due to relationship issues.

These were real people facing real problems who just happened to be in the public eye. As I listened to them, I couldn't help but think of the amazing individuals on my friends list: the coaches, therapists and consultants who have the power to transform lives. What if these celebrities had access to my network? What if the people I know, with their incredible skills and expertise, could help these celebs in a way that no one else could? What if by working with just one of these high-profile clients, they could not only change that person's life but catapult their own business to a whole new level?

I'm writing this book to let you know there's is a huge world outside of social media, a world where your talents, your expertise and your ability to create change are desperately needed. Sure, *Forbes* articles and TV interviews are great, but they're just one piece of the puzzle. They are the parts you can DIY or even outsource if you have the patience and tenacity. But what about the parts that aren't so easy to DIY? What about connecting directly with the type of client whose transformation will pre-sell multiple ideal clients? What about being in the rooms where these conversations happen?

That is where 'done-for-you' PR becomes unparalleled. PR is about people. It is about making connections that matter, ones that can change the entire trajectory of your business. Imagine attending red carpet events or private parties where you're perceived as valuable by the very audience you wish to attract. One celebrity client can change everything not just for your business but for your own sense of purpose and fulfilment. Helping someone who already influences countless others daily means you're not just making a difference; you are making a global impact.

But here's the thing: none of this happens by accident. It requires a strategic approach, one that goes beyond just getting your name in lights. It is about building authority, establishing high-value connections and positioning yourself in a way that no number of business strategies, Facebook ads or media appearances alone can achieve.

STEPPING INTO THE SPOTLIGHT

So what's holding you back? Is it fear? Is it the idea that PR and visibility are for other people, people who are somehow more qualified, more special, more deserving? Perhaps you think the idea of celebrity is déclassé. Let me tell you something: the world needs what you have to offer. There are people out there – high-profile clients, everyday individuals and everyone in between – who are looking for exactly what you provide. But they won't find you if you don't step into the spotlight.

It is time to battle those fears or judgements and take a leap of faith. It is time to put yourself forward as the expert you already are because, the truth is, you're not just doing this for yourself; you are doing it for all the people who need you but don't yet know you exist. If there's one thing I've learned, it's that the most profound impact often comes from the most unexpected places.

Here's to battling our fears together. Here's to making a difference, one connection at a time. Here's to the journey we're about to embark on, one that's filled with purpose, potential and, yes, a little bit of fame because, in the end, it's not about being in the spotlight for the sake of it; it is about using that light to illuminate the path for others.

1
THE ORIGINS OF CELEBRITY
FROM REVERED ICONS TO MODERN-DAY FAME

When we think of celebrities, we likely to conjure up images of Hollywood stars, pop icons and social media influencers with millions of followers and an equally vast fortune. However, the concept of celebrity is far from a modern invention. In fact, the origins of celebrity can be traced back centuries, and understanding this history provides invaluable insight into the role of fame in our world today.

THE EARLY DAYS OF CELEBRITY: REVERENCE AND CONTRIBUTION

In ancient times, the concept of celebrity was intertwined with reverence and respect for individuals who made significant contributions to society. Think about the great philosophers of Ancient Greece like Socrates, Plato and Aristotle. These figures weren't celebrities in the modern sense, but they were well-known and celebrated for their intellectual contributions and their impact on society. Their fame wasn't based on their appearance or their lifestyle but rather on the profound ideas they introduced to the world.

Similarly, during the Renaissance, artists like Leonardo da Vinci and Michelangelo were revered not just for their extraordinary talents but for how their work contributed to the cultural and intellectual growth of society. Their fame was a reflection of their genius and their ability to push the boundaries of what was possible in art and science.

In these early days, celebrity was synonymous with greatness, and to be celebrated was to be recognised for one's contributions to the greater good. The public admired these figures for what they gave to the world, whether it was through art, philosophy or leadership.

THE EVOLUTION OF CELEBRITY: FROM CONTRIBUTIONS TO COMMODITIES

As society evolved, so too did the concept of celebrity. The Industrial Revolution and the advent of mass media played crucial roles in transforming how fame was perceived and created. With the rise of newspapers, radio and eventually television, the ability to reach and influence a large audience became easier and more widespread.

During the 20th century, Hollywood emerged as a powerhouse of celebrity culture. Actors and actresses became household names not necessarily because of their contributions to society, but because of their ability to entertain and captivate the public. The advent of the silver screen turned ordinary people into stars and the public's fascination with their lives, both on and off the screen, grew. Fame became something that could be manufactured, and celebrity became a commodity that could be bought and sold.

This shift marked a significant departure from the days when fame was a result of one's contributions to society. Instead, celebrity became more about visibility, marketability and, often, scandal. The public's interest in the personal lives of celebrities began to outweigh their interest in their professional accomplishments, leading to a culture where being famous for being famous became a reality.

THE MODERN-DAY CELEBRITY: FAME IN THE AGE OF SOCIAL MEDIA

Fast forward to today, and the landscape of celebrity has transformed yet again, largely due to the rise of social media. Platforms like Instagram, TikTok and YouTube have birthed a new breed of celebrities: those who have built their fame from the ground up, often with nothing more than a smartphone and an internet connection. These influencers, as they are commonly known, have mastered the art of connecting with their audience in a way that feels personal and authentic, even as they reach millions.

However, in some ways, the focus on visibility and virality has overshadowed the importance of meaningful contribution. The modern celebrity might be someone who dances well, applies makeup expertly or has a knack for creating engaging content, but the question remains: what lasting impact are they making?

A RETURN TO ROOTS: THE FUTURE OF CELEBRITY

While the nature of celebrity has changed over the centuries, I believe we're on the brink of a shift, a return to the idea that celebrities should be celebrated not just for their visibility but for their contributions to the world. In a society increasingly disillusioned with superficiality, there is a growing demand for authenticity, substance and positive impact.

The future of celebrity, as I envision it, will be one where individuals are recognised and celebrated for the real difference they make. We are seeing the early signs of this shift in the rise of thought leaders, activists and innovators who are using their platforms to drive social change, spread awareness about important issues and inspire others to make a difference.

Imagine a world where the celebrities of tomorrow are those who, like the great thinkers and artists of the past, use their influence to contribute to the betterment of society, where fame is not just a fleeting moment of glory but a reflection of one's commitment to making a lasting impact. This is the kind of celebrity culture I believe we should aspire to come back to.

CONCLUSION: CELEBRATING FOR THE RIGHT REASONS

The history of celebrity shows us that fame has always been a powerful force, capable of shaping public opinion and influencing the course of society, but as we move forward, it's crucial to remember that with great power comes great responsibility.

I believe that by shifting our focus back to celebrating true contributions, we can create a culture where we celebrate those who are not just visible but valuable, those who use their platforms to elevate others, share knowledge and contribute to the world in meaningful ways.

2

THE TRANSFORMATIVE POWER OF FAME AND CELEBRITY

"It is not about what you know, it's not even about who you know; it is about who knows you and for what"

– Brenda Gabriel

In today's world, expertise and connections alone aren't enough to make a lasting impact. You can be the most knowledgeable person in your field and have an extensive network but if people don't know who you are and what you stand for, you'll remain in the shadows. The true power lies in visibility: being recognised and remembered by the right people for the right reasons. This is where the magic of public relations (PR) and personal branding comes into play.

When people know you for your unique value proposition – whether that's your expertise, your innovative approach or the change you're advocating for – they start to associate your name with solutions. You become the go-to person in your industry, the expert whose opinion matters and the leader whose actions inspire. This recognition doesn't just happen by accident; it is carefully cultivated through strategic PR efforts that ensure your message reaches the right ears and resonates in the right hearts.

This concept is critical for anyone looking to build a lasting legacy. Being known for what you do best creates opportunities that otherwise wouldn't have existed. Doors open that were previously closed, conversations start that you weren't a part of before and, suddenly, your influence expands beyond your immediate circle. It's this recognition, this awareness of who you are and what you stand for, that propels you into rooms where decisions are made, where change is initiated and where legacies are built.

In 2019, during a transformative medicine retreat, I received a revelation about my purpose: to create space at the table for those who deserve a seat but can't pull one up for themselves. At that retreat, I was the only Black person, and despite the positive experience, I still felt like an outsider. Not because of my skin colour, but due to cultural differences, much like how a 'Swiftie' might feel at an Erykah Badu concert. My ego whispered, "God, are you sure? I don't want to be the angry Black woman with a chip on my shoulder." But the response I received was clear: "Your mission transcends race; your role is to pave the way for anyone unable to pull up a chair to the table they need to be heard at."

This message has stayed with me, guiding my work in helping people – especially women – shed the limitations imposed by generations of social conditioning and build their own platforms through PR and wealth generation. It is about more than just equality; it is about leveraging PR to create new playing fields where no one is dependent on being allowed onto someone else's to win.

With the advent of social media, it has become easier to imagine a world where anyone with access can become their own media centre. Since 2019, I've dedicated myself to helping those with a desire for positive change get into the right rooms to make the difference they were born to make.

In my years on this planet – 21 (ahem!) recurring – and over a decade working in PR, one universal truth remains: fame and celebrity are two of the most powerful tools for effecting change in the world. Outside of money, fame and celebrity are the most potent influencers that can shape opinions, drive movements and mobilise resources on a global scale. Fame can get you into rooms money never will.

Whether it's raising awareness for a product, pushing for political or legal reform or inspiring cultural shifts, the reach and impact of a well-known figure are unmatched. In today's digital age, where social media and instant communication reign supreme, the influence of fame and celebrity has only grown stronger, making them indispensable assets for anyone – including you – looking to make a meaningful impact on the world.

Let's consider the success stories of Kim Kardashian, who brought global attention to U.S. criminal justice reform and successfully campaigned for the early release of a grandmother; Marcus Rashford, the Premier League footballer who helped raise millions to feed vulnerable children during the pandemic; and comedian Celeste Barber, whose viral fundraiser during the Australian bushfires raised over $51 million. Their celebrity status provided them with platforms, reach and influence that most could only dream of, allowing them to speak directly to world leaders, galvanise public action and influence international policy. Their fame drew significant media attention that translated into real-world support and funding.

Celebrity involvement in a cause almost always puts it firmly in the spotlight, legitimising it in the eyes of the public and encouraging others to engage.

What does this have to do with you as an entrepreneur, executive, artist or influencer? If you believe you're here to make a difference in the world, quite a lot. Leveraging celebrity influence can help your message reach millions, enabling you to drive significant social change. Like it or loathe it, celebrity sells. People are influenced by those they admire and trust, making celebrity endorsement one of the most powerful tools for enhancing the credibility and relevance of any message.

But fame is not just about getting yourself or your business in the spotlight; it is about being seen in the right way, by the right people, at the right time. Fame is about creating life-changing opportunities and leveraging your influence to make a meaningful impact. Fame and celebrity possess a unique power to shape public opinion, drive social movements and create substantial change. In this chapter, we'll explore how you can harness this power to further your goals and amplify your impact.

EVERYBODY WANTS FAME BUT NO ONE WANTS TO BE FAMOUS

If PR has bad PR, fame and celebrity have it even worse. Whenever I discuss PR and my desire to leverage publicity to bring unconventional wisdom, transformational modalities and undercover heroes to the masses, I'm often told that this doesn't come across on social media. I get it. When I talk about celebrity and fame, people often don't hear anything beyond their preconceived notions. Where others use terms like 'visibility' or 'raising profile', I talk in terms of fame and celebrity, which tends to freak people out.

The way I see it is this: anyone who desires greater visibility and recognition has a desire for fame. I am not just talking about the glitz and glamour of red carpets and paparazzi; I am talking about having your name be synonymous with your area of expertise and the solutions your clients are seeking. Just as Coca-Cola is to soft drinks, I want you to be the go-to in your industry.

Fame and celebrity are like ultimate superpowers that help you avoid the barriers to entry that regular people face when it comes to reaching, engaging and growing a global audience. The problem is that it's okay to become accidentally famous, but it's not okay to say that you want to be famous.

Remember when Kim Kardashian was criticised for saying she always wanted to be famous? She has certainly had the last laugh, but it took a long time for her to live that down.

I understand you may have no desire to be 'famous-famous', and that's fine, but let's be real, you don't really have a problem with people becoming aware of your existence based on your work or contribution. After all, to help people, they need to be able to find you, right?

When most people think about becoming famous in their industry, the most common objection is the fear of becoming too famous – viral fame, increased scrutiny or loss of privacy.

Do you know the name of the twentieth most successful person in your industry? Are they always in the papers or on red carpets? Yet, they're likely generating substantial income while making an impact. Just as with Hollywood, there are levels to fame. Not everyone can be the Jennifer Aniston or Tom Cruise of their industry, nor would everyone want to be. It is totally possible to become the go-to expert in your niche within a niche.

When was the last time Richard Branson or one of the Dragons from Dragon's Den was chased by paparazzi? There are levels to fame and notoriety. If you don't want to be an A-list entrepreneur, you don't have to be. You get to choose your level of fame based on how much of an impact you want to make.

The likelihood of toppling Tony Robbins, Gabrielle Bernstein, Patti Stanger or Julia Hart off their podiums is slim. Even then, a twelve-month PR retainer won't do it. Lasting fame requires continuous effort and certainly doesn't happen overnight.

Many successful businesses have never made the press yet are still famous within their own audience in their corner of the market. It is entirely possible to be successful and a relative nobody in celebrity terms. Conversely, fame and celebrity can be leveraged by a business or personal brand for greater reach and impact. Fame and notoriety are not about the person who possesses them; they are about the number of lives you can impact.

FAME AND ITS POTENTIAL FOR WORLD CHANGE

Fame is more than just public recognition; it's an energetic force that can be harnessed for positive change.

By aligning your personal brand with your values and purpose, you can use your influence to inspire and lead others. Fame, when approached with integrity and intention, becomes a powerful tool for driving social change and making a lasting impact.

Fame is like a magnifying glass: it doesn't create anything new; it simply makes what's already there, more visible. This means it can magnify your strengths, your passions and, unfortunately, your flaws too. The public gaze can be relentless and unforgiving, but it also offers an unparalleled opportunity to showcase your true self and your mission to the world.

When you embrace fame with a clear understanding of your purpose, you can navigate its challenges and use it as a vehicle for profound, positive transformation. Think of fame as an amplifier of your inner energy. If you're grounded in your values and purpose, fame can project that positive energy out into the world, influencing and inspiring countless others.

WHY SHOULD YOU CARE?

I strongly believe that understanding the power of fame and celebrity can help you craft a strategic approach to your PR efforts. It encourages you to think beyond traditional PR tactics and consider how you can use your unique influence to create meaningful change. This perspective not only enhances your personal brand but contributes to a greater legacy, one that resonates long after the spotlight has moved on.

Fame isn't just about being known; it is about being known for something that matters. It is about having a platform to amplify messages that can change lives, shift perspectives and drive social movements. When you align your fame with your core values and mission, you become a beacon of authenticity and integrity, drawing people who resonate with your message and are inspired to join your cause.

I can't tell you how many people I've met who say they have no interest in fame and celebrity yet spend time watching, reading about or buying from notable people every single day. What makes them any more noteworthy than you? I will tell you what: absolutely nothing.

In truth, we all want to be famous with the right people for our work, just on our terms. I am here to tell you that it's totally possible.

I don't believe it's possible to serve at your highest possible level if anyone who needs to know about you doesn't, which is why PR and publicity aren't just nice to have; they are essential tools in the arsenal of anyone who aims to have a global impact.

Let's delve deeper into the celebrity-led initiatives mentioned earlier and examine how the level of influence, audience size and notoriety of these public figures correlates with the significant impact they were able to achieve. If you engage in any sort of media, it's likely you remember reading or hearing about at least one of these initiatives, even if you don't live in the same country as where the news took place. At least two of these initiatives made global news, not just local or national, demonstrating the bigger the profile, the bigger the influence.

KIM KARDASHIAN — CRIMINAL JUSTICE REFORM

Kim Kardashian's involvement in criminal justice reform is a prime example of how celebrity power can transcend traditional activism and reach the highest levels of influence. Before her advocacy work, Kardashian was primarily known for her reality TV fame and massive social media following, boasting over 200 million followers across platforms like Instagram and Twitter. This level of reach is challenged only by the reach of traditional media in its ability to disseminate information quickly and to a broad audience.

In 2018, Kardashian learned about Alice Marie Johnson, a grandmother serving a life sentence without parole for a nonviolent drug offence. Kardashian's initial tweet about Johnson's case immediately garnered widespread attention. However, it was her personal meeting with then-President Donald Trump that truly showcased the extent of her influence. Within days of their meeting, Trump commuted Johnson's sentence, leading to her release after twenty-one years in prison.

Kardashian's notoriety allowed her to bypass traditional bureaucratic barriers. Her ability to connect with influential figures like the president, combined with her massive audience, transformed her from a reality TV star into a powerful advocate for justice reform. The media coverage of her involvement was extensive, with major news outlets around the world reporting on her advocacy. This sustained attention not only led to Johnson's release but sparked broader conversations about sentencing reform and the potential for further legislative changes. Kardashian's influence didn't just stop at a single case; it opened doors for continued dialogue on a national scale, demonstrating how celebrity status can be leveraged to effect real, systemic change.

A woman who gained fame as a reality TV star was able to not only change the life of a woman and her family but that of potentially millions of people across the US because her actions were able to spark conversation.

MARCUS RASHFORD — CHILD FOOD SECURITY

Marcus Rashford, a Premier League footballer playing for Manchester United, used his platform to address a deeply personal issue: child food security. Growing up in a low-income household, Rashford had firsthand experience of the struggles many families face in providing adequate nutrition for their children. By 2020, Rashford had become not only a sports icon with millions of fans but a vocal advocate for social justice.

During the COVID-19 pandemic, Rashford launched a campaign to extend free school meals for vulnerable children during the holidays, a time when many families would struggle the most. His open letter to the UK government, combined with a social media campaign that reached millions, put immense pressure on policymakers. Rashford's tweets alone garnered millions of engagements, and his interviews and public appearances kept the issue in the spotlight.

Rashford's efforts led to a dramatic policy reversal by the UK government, which initially refused to extend the programme. The government's eventual U-turn and subsequent extension of the free school meals programme can be directly attributed to the public pressure Rashford generated. The media coverage of his campaign was widespread, from national newspapers to international news outlets, all highlighting not just his footballing prowess but his commitment to social change.

Moreover, Rashford's campaign raised over £20 million, which helped feed millions of children across the UK. His work didn't stop with the pandemic; he continued to advocate for systemic changes to address child poverty, meeting with policymakers and experts to discuss long-term solutions. Rashford's influence, grounded in both his celebrity status and his authentic connection to the cause, demonstrated how a well-known figure could mobilise public opinion and drive significant government action.

CELESTE BARBER — AUSTRALIAN BUSHFIRE RELIEF

Comedian Celeste Barber leveraged her social media following to create one of the most successful online fundraising campaigns in history. Known for her humorous takes on celebrity culture, Barber had amassed a substantial following, with millions of fans across Instagram and Facebook by the time the devastating Australian bushfires began in late 2019.

When Barber started her fundraiser on Facebook, her initial goal was modest: to raise $30,000 AUD. However, within days, the campaign went viral thanks to Barber's influence and the global reach of her social media platforms. People around the world were drawn to her authenticity and the personal connection she had to the fires affecting her home country. The fundraiser quickly gained attraction, and in just over a week, Barber had raised more than $51 million AUD, an extraordinary amount that far surpassed any previous fundraising efforts for the crisis.

The massive media attention that followed further amplified the campaign. News outlets globally reported on Barber's efforts, and her campaign became a symbol of grassroots mobilisation in response to a disaster. The funds raised were used to support fire services, communities affected by the fires and wildlife rescue efforts.

Barber's widespread appeal, combined with her strategic use of social media, showcased how a celebrity's platform could be used not just for entertainment but for substantial, life-saving efforts. The success of her campaign highlighted the potential for celebrities to harness their notoriety and influence for good, reaching far beyond their usual audiences to effect real-world change.

THE POWER OF CELEBRITY IN DRIVING CHANGE

The size of the audience, the level of influence and the ability to connect with both the public and those in power were all critical factors in the success of these initiatives. Over and above the significant media coverage received by these acts, we saw firsthand how fame and celebrity can be leveraged not just for personal gain, but to transform the lives of others.

Kim Kardashian's ability to influence the highest levels of government, Marcus Rashford's success in changing public policy and Celeste Barber's record-breaking fund-raising campaign all underscore the unique power of celebrity. When celebrities align their influence with meaningful causes, they have the potential to not only raise awareness but drive action, shift public opinion and create tangible outcomes. This is the true power of fame.

In the chapters that follow, we will dive deep into what PR actually is and what its benefits are in terms that make sense to you, and the best ways to forge and leverage relationships along with fame and celebrity to achieve your goals. We will explore practical strategies, share insights from successful campaigns and guide you on a journey to becoming a conscious celebrity, one who uses their platform for good and inspires others to do the same.

We will talk about the importance of authenticity, integrity and staying true to your values on the journey, how to build a lasting legacy and how to leverage your influence to create a ripple effect that extends far beyond your immediate circle.

QUESTIONS FOR REFLECTION:

What Does Fame Mean to You?

How do you define fame and celebrity? Are these things you aspire to, or do they feel daunting? What are your reasons for wanting (or avoiding) fame?

What Impact Do You Want to Make?

How do you want to use your influence? Think about the social, cultural or industry changes you want to drive. How could fame help you achieve these goals?

Are You Prepared for the Challenges of Fame?

Fame brings scrutiny and pressure. Are you mentally and emotionally prepared to handle the attention and expectations that come with being a public figure?

Who Are Your Role Models?

Which celebrities or influential figures do you admire? What can you learn from their journey to fame, both their successes and their challenges?

What Is Your Unique Message?

What makes you and your brand unique? How can you communicate this uniqueness in a way that resonates with a broad audience?

POINTS TO CONSIDER:

The Dual Nature of Fame:

Fame can amplify both your strengths and your weaknesses. Consider how you will manage the dual aspects of visibility, celebrating your successes while also handling any publicised flaws or mistakes.

Using Fame for Good:

Fame isn't just about recognition; it is a tool for change. Think about how you can leverage your platform to promote causes you care about and make a positive impact on society.

Levels of Fame:

Not all fame is equal. Consider what level of fame you're comfortable with. Do you want to be a household name, or are you aiming for niche recognition within your industry?

Sustainable Fame:

Quick fame can be fleeting. Reflect upon how you can build a lasting presence that endures beyond momentary trends or viral moments. What steps can you take to ensure your influence grows over time?

Aligning Fame with Purpose:

Fame is most powerful when it's aligned with your true purpose. Think about how your personal values and mission can guide your journey to becoming a recognised and respected figure.

These questions and points will help you to think more deeply about the role that fame and celebrity can play in your life and how you can strategically and intentionally pursue fame in a way that aligns with your values and goals.

3

WHAT EVEN IS PR ANYWAY?
(IN LAYMAN'S TERMS)

"If a young man tells his date how handsome, smart and successful he is, that's advertising. If the young man tells his date she's intelligent, looks lovely and is a great conversationalist, he's saying the right things to the right person, and that's marketing. If someone else tells the young woman how handsome, smart and successful her date is, that's PR."

– Sylvia H. Simmons

This quote is one of the best ways I've come across explaining the difference between PR advertising and marketing in a clear, succinct way.

Ask the average person what PR actually means, and you're likely to get a range of responses, from "getting on the news" to "spinning the truth." But here's the thing: PR is so much more than just media coverage or manipulating the narrative; it is about managing how the world sees you, your brand or your business, and that encompasses everything from your social media presence to your customer reviews, your events and even your partnerships.

Over the years, countless experts have tried with a limited degree of success to define and sum up PR. Nailing down a one-size-fits-all definition has proven to be a bit like trying to catch a cloud in a jar: just when you think you have it, it slips away. PR can be tricky like that, not least because it encompasses a wide range of activities and strategies that can vary drastically depending on who or what is being 'PR'd', so to speak.

So What Is PR Again?

The **Chartered Institute of Public Relations (CIPR)** gives a definition as follows:

"Public relations is about reputation – the result of what you do, what you say and what others say about you. It is the discipline which looks after reputation, with the aim of earning understanding and support and influencing opinion and behaviour."

While the **Public Relations Society of America (PRSA) states**:

"Public relations is a strategic communication process that builds mutually beneficial relationships between organisations and their publics."

Both definitions encapsulate the essence of PR, which is essentially strategic communication, relationship building and reputation management.

If even the professionals can't agree on a single definition, is it any wonder you're likely confused about what it is beyond getting in the news, and exactly how it will benefit you beyond seeing your face in print?

Ask ten PR pros what PR really is, and you'll get ten different answers, ranging from "getting you on TV" to "making sure your brand has a soul." The truth is, PR is all of these things and more. It is about managing how the world sees you, whether that's through traditional media, social media or even blogs.

At its essence, public relations (PR) is the art of storytelling: crafting and sharing your story with the world in a way that makes them feel a connection with you, building trust and fostering meaningful relationships with your audience. It is about managing and curating your public image, deciding the parts of your story you wish to share and leveraging your increased visibility, platform, authority and credibility to influence public perception. Whether you're an entrepreneur, an artist or a business owner, PR is your way of telling the world who you are, what you stand for and why they should care.

PR isn't just about traditional media like newspapers, TV or radio; it is about everything someone experiences about your brand, from your website and social media profiles to the events you host and the collaborations you engage in. It is the positive reviews, the customer testimonials, the partnerships and, yes, the awards you win. All of these elements contribute to your public image and influence how people perceive you.

The truth is, PR is a broad and flexible field, which is part of what makes it so powerful yet challenging to grasp. Depending on the brand, the message to be communicated, the audience and the desired outcomes, the methods or approach to achieving this can be highly fluid and totally subjective.

PR is a bit of a nebulous concept that often feels intangible. This stems from the need for the strategy around it to be adaptable. Due to the ever-shifting nature of communication, PR and those who deliver it have to constantly evolve with new media platforms and cultural shifts. For instance, tactics that work in traditional media may not translate well to social media, and vice versa.

Imagine you're launching a new product: a high-end, jewelled, eco-friendly water bottle. Now, if you're going the traditional PR route, you might pitch the story to a respected lifestyle magazine such as Cosmo, Vogue or a national newspaper. They might run a feature about how your product is revolutionising the way people stay hydrated while saving the planet. This kind of coverage in a trusted publication can give your brand a significant credibility boost, especially with an audience that values in-depth reporting and editorial integrity.

However, the same approach might not work as well on social media. On platforms like Instagram or TikTok, where the audience is more visually driven and content moves at lightning speed, you'll need a different tactic. Instead of a lengthy article, you might partner with influencers who can create eye-catching shorts or reels showcasing the water bottle's design and eco-friendly benefits. Here, it's all about quick, engaging content that grabs attention within seconds.

While traditional media coverage builds your brand's credibility and trust among a certain demographic, the social media campaign generates buzz and drives immediate engagement among a younger or more visually-oriented crowd. These tactics are different, but both are crucial parts of a comprehensive PR strategy.

This example demonstrates the need for adaptability in PR. The key to implementing a successful campaign is understanding where your target audience is and how they consume content, then tailoring your approach to meet them where they are.

Traditional PR tends to work well alongside social media, both mediums having a sort of symbiosis in which one compliments and amplifies the other.

Now, in order to truly understand where you're going, I believe it's essential to know where you've been. In order to understand the relevance of PR to you today, I think it's worth sharing a brief history lesson.

THE HISTORY OF PR – A WALK DOWN MEMORY LANE

THE EARLY DAYS: ANCIENT CIVILISATIONS TO THE 19TH CENTURY

Let's take a little trip back in time. Public relations, or 'PR' as we lovingly call it, has been around longer than you might think. In fact, it's been lurking in the shadows of human history since ancient times. Imagine, way back in ancient Greece and Rome, there were these smooth-talking orators and rhetoricians who were basically the original PR pros. They were hired by big-shot leaders to sway public opinion and win over the masses. These guys were the masters of spin before 'spin' was even a thing.

Fast forward to the Middle Ages, and you'll find that even the Catholic Church was getting in on the PR action. They used symbols, rituals and grand proclamations to keep their influence strong. The Church knew that managing public perception was key to maintaining power, a lesson that holds true even today.

Now, let's jump ahead to the 18th century, where things start to get really interesting. In the U.S., during the American Revolution, a guy named Thomas Paine used pamphlets and essays to rally the public for independence. His pamphlet *Common Sense* was like the viral tweet of its day, spreading like wildfire and making a massive impact. This was one of the earliest examples of PR being used for a political cause, and it worked like a charm.

THE BIRTH OF MODERN PR: ENTER THE FOUNDING FATHERS

But the real birth of modern PR as we know it came in the early 20th century. Meet Ivy Lee, one of the OGs of PR. Ivy was hired by John D. Rockefeller to clean up a bit of a mess – okay, a big mess – known as the Ludlow Massacre, where striking workers were killed. Ivy didn't just sweep things under the rug (which, let's be honest, would've been the go-to move back then). Instead, he advised Rockefeller to be transparent, communicate directly with the public and even go visit the miners' families. Radical, right? This approach was a game-changer and laid the groundwork for what we consider ethical PR today.

Then there's Edward Bernays, another PR pioneer and the nephew of Sigmund Freud. Bernays took things to the next level by applying psychology to PR. He realised that you could shape public opinion much like you could nudge someone into a new habit. He is also the guy who pretty much invented the term 'public relations' and wrote the book on it. Literally. His book *Crystallizing Public Opinion* is still a must-read for PR nerds everywhere.

One of Bernays' most famous stunts was the 'Torches of Freedom' campaign, where he convinced women to smoke cigarettes publicly during a New York parade. It was a bold move that not only challenged societal norms but sent tobacco sales soaring. Not exactly a public health win, but a PR masterstroke nonetheless.

THE GOLDEN AGE OF PR: LIGHTS, CAMERA, ACTION!

The mid-20th century was the golden age of PR. As radio, TV and print media became the go-to sources for news and entertainment, PR pros found themselves in high demand. Corporations realised that having a good PR team was just as important as having a solid product. It was all about crafting the perfect image and managing public perception.

This was also the era when PR started to play a huge role in politics. The invention of television transformed political campaigns. Candidates now had to look good on screen and be able to connect with voters through the lens of a camera. PR experts became the unsung heroes behind many political successes, coaching candidates on everything from what to say to how to smile.

By the 1980s, PR had fully cemented itself as a crucial part of both business and celebrity culture. This was the time when PR legends like Richard Edelman and Howard Rubenstein rose to fame, shaping the images of everyone from Fortune 500 companies to Hollywood stars.

THE DIGITAL REVOLUTION: THE INTERNET CHANGES EVERYTHING

Then came the internet and with it a whole new world for PR. The late 20th century brought us email, websites and the first glimmers of social media. Suddenly, brands could communicate directly with their audiences without needing to go through traditional media. This was both a blessing and a curse. On one hand, it gave brands more control over their messaging. On the other hand, it also meant that any mistake could go viral in a heartbeat.

The rise of 24/7 news cycles and social media also meant that PR had to become more reactive and agile. A PR crisis could now unfold in real time with the whole world watching. This made crisis management a top priority for PR pros everywhere.

THE SOCIAL MEDIA ERA: EVERYONE IS A MEDIA CENTRE

The last decade has been all about social media. Platforms like Facebook, Twitter, Instagram and TikTok have democratised media, making it possible for anyone with a smartphone to become an influencer. Brands no longer need to rely solely on traditional media to get their message out; they can now build their own audiences directly.

These days, you can build an empire without ever setting foot in a TV studio. Just look at major influencers who've made it big purely through social media. Some of them have never done a single interview on television yet have millions of followers hanging on their every word. Take Belle du Jour, a blogger who started writing about her experiences anonymously, only to see her blog blow up so much that it was eventually turned into a book and then a TV show. All of this happened without the traditional media push that most people associate with 'making it'.

With this said, the sheer volume of content being produced on social media means that it's harder than ever to stand out.

The speed at which information travels on social media has forced PR professionals to be more nimble. A single tweet can go viral within minutes, requiring immediate responses to manage public perception.

INTEGRATED PR: BRINGING IT ALL TOGETHER

Today, PR is all about integration. The days of relying solely on traditional media are long gone. Modern PR requires a blend of media relations, digital strategies, content creation and influencer partnerships. Enter the PESO model, a brilliant framework developed by PR expert Gini Dietrich.

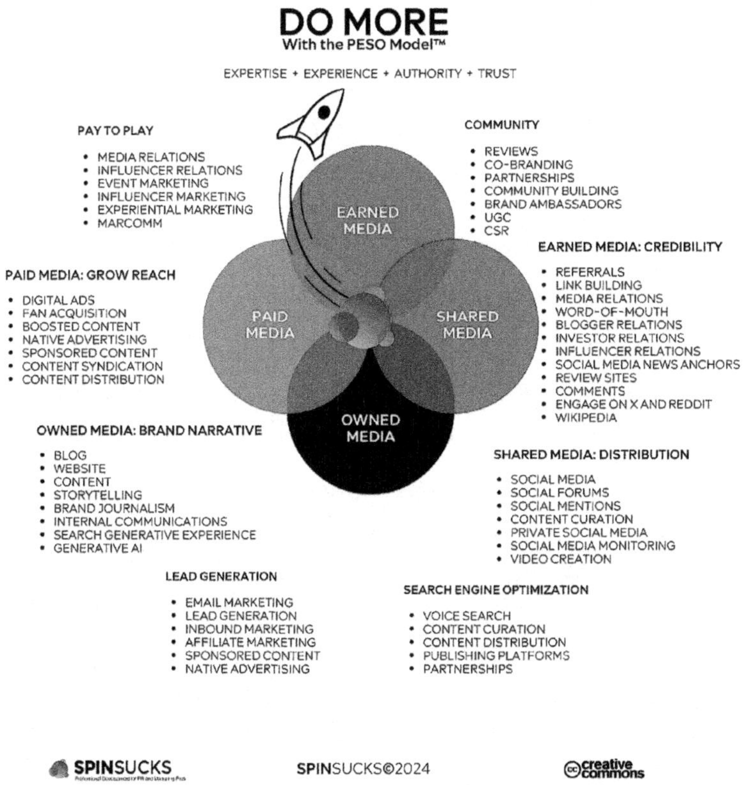

Paid Media: Think social media ads and sponsored content. It's about getting your message out to as many people as possible.

Earned Media: This is your bread and butter – getting journalists and bloggers to cover your story without paying them.

Shared Media: Your social media playground. It is where you build a community and get people talking about your brand.

Owned Media: Your domain – blogs, websites, newsletters. Here, you have full control over your message.

The beauty of the PESO model is that it allows for a cohesive strategy that touches all the bases. It is about making sure your message is consistent across all channels, so whether someone finds you through a blog post, a tweet or a magazine article, they're getting the same story.

As we move forward, PR will continue to evolve with new technologies and platforms, but at its core, it will always be about storytelling and managing how the world sees you.

Now that you understand how the PR landscape has changed, let's look at how it differs from the other kids on the marketing block.

KEY DIFFERENCES BETWEEN PR, PAID MEDIA, MARKETING AND ADVERTISING

Now, let's clear up some confusion. PR, advertising and marketing often get lumped together like one big, happy family, but they're actually more like sisters: related, but each with their own personality. Here is a brief explanation of the differences:

PR: PR is all about earning your place in the spotlight. It is about building relationships, crafting stories that journalists want to cover and managing how the public sees you. Unlike advertising, you're not paying for this coverage; you are earning it through being interesting enough to write about and good old-fashioned hustle.

Advertising: This is the part of the family that has no problem paying to be heard. Whether it's a TV commercial, a print ad or a sponsored post on Instagram, advertising is direct and in your face. The downside? People know you're paying to be there, which can make them a bit sceptical.

Whilst advertising focuses on promoting products or services, PR, just as in anything to do with relationships is more about the subtleties and nuance of engaging with those who matter the most to you and or have a vested interest in you or your brand.

Marketing: Think of marketing as the big umbrella that covers everything from PR to advertising to sales. It is the strategic plan that ties all your promotional efforts together. While PR is about building trust and credibility, marketing is more about driving sales and making sure people know they need what you're selling.

When it comes to PR vs paid media, the lines are completely blurred for most, so many people are mis-sold paid media as traditional PR. The lack of transparency around it is something that drives me absolutely spare! This includes many of the AI 'PR' tools on the market selling AI-generated, pay-to-play press releases as thought leadership PR.

As shown by the PESO model, paid media does have its place in a well-thought-out, integrated PR strategy, but it doesn't replace high-quality earned coverage. The inability to 'buy' this PR is the primary reason it's so valuable. Paid-for coverage is not the same nor does it have the same credibility as PR no matter how it's positioned. Paid PR may enhance earned coverage, but it cannot replace it.

Just so we're clear, If you have to pay the outlet to appear, it's paid media, not earned PR.

Understanding these differences is like knowing when to use a spoon instead of a fork: it is crucial for getting the job done right. PR can enhance your marketing efforts by building trust and credibility, which makes your advertising more effective. It is all connected, but knowing what tool to use and when is key.

UNDERSTANDING MEDIA CHANNELS AND THEIR UNIQUE ADVANTAGES

Let's talk about the many ways you can get your message out there. In today's media landscape, you've got options, and knowing the strengths of each can help you craft a killer PR strategy.

- **Traditional Media (Print, TV, Radio):** These guys are the old guard, but don't count them out just yet. Getting a mention in a respected newspaper, magazine or TV show can give your brand a serious credibility boost. Plus, older or more traditional audiences still trust these sources more than what they read on Facebook.
- **Digital Media (Blogs, Online News, Podcasts):** This is where things get flexible and fun. Digital media allows you to target niche audiences and get your message out there without needing a massive advertising budget. Plus, the internet never sleeps, so your content can reach people anytime, anywhere.
- **Social Media (Facebook, Instagram, Twitter, LinkedIn):** Social media is where you get to roll up your sleeves and engage with your audience directly. It is real time, it's interactive and it's where you can turn your followers into brand advocates. Plus, it's a great way to amplify your PR efforts by getting your audience to do some of the heavy lifting for you.
- **Influencers and Thought Leaders:** Partnering with influencers or thought leaders can be like getting a VIP pass to your audience's hearts. These folks already have the trust and admiration of their followers, so their endorsement can go a long way. Just make sure you're picking the right partners, ones who align with your brand values.

Each of these channels has its own vibe, and a savvy PR strategy will mix and match them to reach the right people in the right way.

THE ROLE OF PR IN SHAPING PUBLIC PERCEPTION

At the end of the day, PR is all about perception. It is about making sure that when people think of you or your brand, they think of something positive, trustworthy and worth their time. It is about managing your reputation, handling crises like a pro and keeping your message consistent across all platforms.

PR can help you become a thought leader in your industry, build trust with your audience and open doors to new opportunities. It is not just about getting your name out there; it is about getting your name out there in a way that builds relationships, fosters trust and, ultimately, drives growth.

Now that we're clear on what PR is (and isn't), let's look at one of the biggest benefits of it: third-party endorsement.

THE PERKS OF PR FOR YOU AS A PERSONAL BRAND AND THE IMPORTANCE OF THIRD-PARTY ENDORSEMENT

Now that we've covered the basics of PR, let's take an in depth look at the perks of PR and the magic of third-party endorsements. You might be thinking, "Is PR really worth all the hype?" The answer of course is a resounding yes. PR isn't just about getting your name in lights; it is about creating a powerful, ongoing presence that positions you as, in the immortal word of Queen Bey: "One of one, the only one." Third-party endorsement from earned media is a great way to build trust in you and your brand.

Whenever another person, whether they be a journalist, influencer or happy customer, talks about you, your product or your service in a positive way, it carries a weight that you simply can't achieve through self-promotion alone. It is like them having a trusted friend vouch for you. Suddenly, people are more inclined to listen, trust and engage with what you have to say. This kind of validation can be a game-changer, opening doors you didn't even know existed.

When the media or influencers sing your praises, it's more than free advertising; it is a stamp of approval that tells the world you're the real deal. People are naturally sceptical of brands tooting their own horn, but when that praise comes from someone they already trust and respect, it cuts through the noise. It is not just you saying you're great; someone else with credibility is backing you up.

Third-party endorsements build your credibility, amplify your reach and give you a level of social proof that's hard to buy. It is the difference between telling people you're awesome and having others say it for you. In the world of PR, that difference is everything.

So let's dive deeper into the multitude of ways PR and the third-party endorsements it brings work their magic and how you can leverage these to boost your brand, create lasting relationships and build a rock-solid reputation. Twenty-eight ways, to be exact, because I never want you to question the benefits or value of PR to your personal brand and/or business ever again. Ready?

1. Becoming the Trustworthy Go-To

In the vast world of business, credibility is king. Imagine you're looking for a new hairstylist. Would you trust someone just because they put up a flashy ad, or are you more likely to go for someone who's been recommended by a top beauty magazine and has a portfolio of glowing testimonials? Most of us would go for the latter because we trust the word of others, especially if those 'others' are respected voices in the industry.

PR helps you build that kind of credibility. Whenever your brand is featured in reputable media outlets or endorsed by industry experts, it's like getting a gold star from the world. Your audience see you as a trusted authority and in business, trust is everything. With PR, you're not just telling people you're great; you are showing them through the eyes of trusted third parties.

2. Getting in Front of the Right People

You could be the best-kept secret in your industry, but if no one knows about you, how far will you really go? PR is like a megaphone for your brand, helping you reach a wider and more diverse audience. When a respected media outlet or an influencer in your niche talks about you, you're suddenly on the radar of their audience too.

This isn't just about numbers; it is about quality. PR doesn't just throw your name out there; it strategically places you in front of the right people, those who are likely to be interested in what you have to offer. Think of it as getting VIP access to the people who matter most to your business.

3. The Stamp of Approval

In a world where anyone can claim to be an expert on social media, how do you stand out? PR gives you that all-important stamp of approval. When industry leaders and respected media outlets validate your expertise, it's like having your credentials certified by the best in the business.

This validation is more than just a confidence boost; it opens doors. Suddenly, you're getting invited to speak at conferences, participate in panels and collaborate with other experts. PR turns you from just another voice into the voice people want to hear.

4. The Mere Exposure Effect

The more people that see or hear about your brand through trusted third parties, the more they begin to like and trust you. This subtle psychological principle works in your favour as repeated exposure builds familiarity and affinity.

5. Humanising your Brand

When others talk about your brand, it gives your business a personality and a human touch. It is not just a logo or a product anymore; it is something people can relate to on a personal level.

6. Parasocial Relationship Building

Third-party endorsements help build a one-sided relationship where audiences feel connected to your brand even if they haven't interacted with you directly. It is like having a fan base that roots for you because they feel they already know you. Understanding parasocial relationships is important when it comes to building and managing your personal brand. They also come with a moral obligation not to exploit the influence they can wield.

7. Working Even When You Don't or Can't

One of the greatest perks of third-party endorsements is that they keep working even when you're not actively promoting yourself. Your brand continues to gain visibility and trust even while you're focusing on other aspects of your business.

8. Non-reliance on a System to Work

Unlike certain marketing efforts that require constant attention and tweaking, third-party endorsements are organic and don't need a specific system or constant management to be effective.

9. Increasing Touch Points in Advance of Connecting with You

Each time someone sees or hears about you from a third-party source, it's like an additional touchpoint in the customer journey. By the time they actually connect with you, they already feel a sense of familiarity and trust.

10. Showcasing Expertise and Knowledge

Third-party endorsements naturally highlight your expertise and knowledge. When someone else vouches for you, it's like a stamp of approval on your skills and authority in your field.

11. Doing Once, Working Forever

The beauty of third-party endorsements is their longevity. A positive mention or review can continue to influence potential customers long after it's been published, unlike ads or social media posts that have a short shelf life.

12. Amplifying Other Marketing Efforts

Third-party endorsements work in tandem with your other marketing strategies, amplifying their effectiveness. They give a boost to your campaigns by adding credibility and an extra layer of trust.

Leveraged/borrowed authority: when a respected third party endorses you, it's like borrowing their authority and credibility. Their endorsement lends weight to your brand, making it more likely that others will trust and engage with you.

13. Everyone Loves a Bandwagon

We've all chosen a restaurant because it's packed while the one next door is empty. That is social proof in action. PR leverages this psychological phenomenon by showcasing your brand in a way that makes others want to jump on board.

When people see you getting media coverage or hear an influencer singing your praises, they're more likely to think, "If everyone else is paying attention, maybe I should too." Social proof isn't just about following the crowd; it is about showing potential customers that you're worth their time and money.

14. Planting Seeds for the Future

One of the most underrated benefits of PR is its ability to fuel long-term growth. Sure, PR can get you immediate attention, but its real power lies in its ability to build a solid foundation for the future. Each media mention, endorsement or partnership is a seed planted in the fertile soil of your brand's reputation. Over time, these seeds grow into a strong, thriving brand that's recognised and respected in your industry.

Consistency is key. When you get third-party endorsements regularly, it helps build trust over time. People start to think, "If these sources keep vouching for this brand, they must be legit." PR is not one and done. Do not be the brand that dines out on that solitary 'one time in band camp' feature on *Forbes* that no one can find because it's over ten years old.

15. Becoming the Benchmark

When your brand is consistently featured in the media and endorsed by respected figures, you're not just competing in your market; you are setting the benchmark. PR helps position you as a leader, someone others in your industry look to for guidance and inspiration.

This kind of positioning doesn't just happen overnight; it is the result of a sustained PR effort that keeps your brand in the public eye, consistently showcasing your expertise and achievements. Over time, you become the standard by which others are measured.

16. Objectivity: the Unbiased Truth Serum

Here is the deal: when an endorsement comes from a third party, it's seen as more objective. It is like getting a thumbs up from the universe. People are naturally sceptical of self-promotion (we've all seen those cringy sales pitches), but when an unbiased source says you're the real deal, it carries way more weight.

17. Reach and Influence: Everyone Loves a Popular Kid

Endorsements from media outlets, influencers or industry bigwigs can open doors to audiences you didn't even know existed. These folks have followers who hang on their every word, so when they give you a shoutout, it's like getting invited to sit at the cool kids' table in the cafeteria. Suddenly, your message is reaching far beyond your usual crowd.

18. Validation: the 'You've Arrived' Moment

There is something about a third-party endorsement that just screams, "You've made it!" It is like when your mum or bestie finally stops asking what you do for a living because they saw your name in a magazine. That external validation shows that your brand or product meets a certain standard and is recognised by people who matter.

19. Amplification: Turn up the Volume

Endorsements aren't just nice to have; they can take your PR game to the next level. You can sprinkle them across your social media, press releases and marketing materials to really drive home your message. It is like turning up the volume on your brand's megaphone.

20. Differentiation: Standing Out in a Sea of Sameness

No matter your industry, you've got competition. But here's the good news: PR helps you stand out. In a crowded market, being different isn't just an advantage; it is essential. PR highlights what makes you unique, whether it's your personal story, your innovative approach or your specific niche.

By telling your story in the media, you differentiate yourself from the competition. You are not just another business owner; you are the business owner with a compelling story that people want to hear, the human element being the kind of thing people remember.

Third-party endorsement can be your secret weapon, highlighting what makes you unique and giving you an edge over your competitors. It is like having a neon sign above your head that says, "I'm the best choice and everyone agrees!"

21. SEO Benefits: Google Loves You

Here's is a bonus for all you SEO nerds out there. When reputable sources mention and link to your brand, it's like getting a high-five from Google. These backlinks can boost your search engine rankings, making it easier for people to find you online. Who doesn't want to be more visible on the world's most popular search engine?

22. Investor Confidence: Show Me the Money

An increasing number of businesses are competing for investment. In addition to great numbers and proof of concept, investors like to see that a company and the founder has credibility and longevity. Third-party endorsements are a great way to demonstrate there's a buzz about and demand for what you do. When industry experts or media outlets and the public are talking about your company, it naturally makes you a more attractive investment.

23. Employee Morale: Pride in the Workplace

Nothing boosts employee morale like seeing their hard work get recognised by respected sources. When your company gets public endorsements, it gives your team something to be proud of. Happy employees are productive employees. Who doesn't want that?

24. Content Marketing: Endless Ammo

Endorsements aren't just a one-time deal; they are content gold. You can repurpose them into case studies, testimonials, blog posts and more. It is like having a bottomless bag of marketing tricks.

25. Consumer Advocacy: Turning Customers into Cheerleaders

When people see that trusted sources endorse your brand, they're more likely to share their positive experiences and recommend you to others. It is like having an army of cheerleaders spreading the good word.

26. Long-Term Relationships: the Gift That Keeps on Giving

Building relationships with third-party endorsers isn't just a one-time thing; these relationships can lead to long-term collaborations that benefit your brand in the long run. Think of it as planting seeds that will grow into mighty oaks.

27. Enhanced Media Relations: Easier Access to the Spotlight

When influential media figures endorse your brand, it strengthens your relationships with journalists and editors. This can lead to more favourable coverage and easier access to media opportunities in the future. It is like getting a backstage pass to the PR world.

28. Crisis Management: a Lifeline When Things Go South

No one likes to think about crises, but they do happen – just ask the Royal Family. When they do, having third-party endorsements can be a lifeline. Support from respected sources can lend credibility to your brand's response and help reassure stakeholders. It is like having a trusted friend vouch for you when you're in a tough spot.

In short (or not), third-party endorsements are the unsung heroes of PR. They add authenticity, boost credibility and can take your brand from 'meh' to 'must-have.' So, next time someone gives you a shoutout, don't just thank them; leverage it!

QUESTIONS FOR REFLECTION:

How Do You Currently Perceive PR?

Before reading this chapter, what was your understanding of PR? How has this understanding evolved after learning about PR in layman's terms?

What Are Your Current PR Efforts?

Are you currently engaging in any PR activities? If so, how effective have they been? If not, what's holding you back from leveraging PR for your brand?

Who Are Your Trusted Third Parties?

Think about the key players in your industry – media outlets, influencers or experts – whose endorsement could add credibility to your brand. How can you start building relationships with them?

What Is Your Brand's Story?

Every brand has a unique story. How well have you communicated your story to your audience? Could PR help in refining and amplifying this narrative?

How Do You Handle Public Perception?

How do you currently manage how the public perceives your brand? Are you proactive in shaping your image, or do you tend to react to situations as they arise?

POINTS TO CONSIDER:

The Importance of Credibility:

PR enhances your brand's credibility by getting others to vouch for you. Reflect upon how third-party endorsements can strengthen your reputation and make your brand more trustworthy in the eyes of your audience.

Objectivity Is Key:

PR works because it provides an objective view of your brand. Consider how having someone else, like a journalist or influencer, talk about your brand might carry more weight than your own self-promotion.

Amplifying Your Message:

One of the biggest advantages of PR is its ability to amplify your message. Think about the ways in which PR can help you reach a larger, more diverse audience by tapping into the networks of respected media outlets and influencers.

Building Trust Through Consistency:

Trust is built over time. Reflect upon how consistent PR efforts – like regular features, interviews or testimonials – can help build long-term trust with your audience, leading to greater loyalty and engagement.

Differentiating Your Brand:

In a crowded market, standing out is crucial. Consider how PR can help differentiate your brand by highlighting what makes you unique and positioning you as a leader in your industry.

These questions and points will help you think critically about how PR can be used as a strategic tool to build credibility, reach new audiences and strengthen your brand's reputation in a meaningful way.

FINAL THOUGHTS: PR AS YOUR BRAND'S BEST FRIEND

In a nutshell, PR is like that friend who always knows the right thing to say, who can get you into the best parties and who's there to support you when things go sideways. It is not just about getting your name out there; it is about building a brand that people trust, admire and want to be associated with.

Whether you're just starting out or you're looking to take your business to the next level, PR is an investment in your brand's future. It is the key to unlocking new opportunities, growing your influence and making a lasting impact in your industry.

So, now that you know why PR is so important for you as a personal brand, it's time to start thinking about how you can leverage it to achieve your goals. In the next chapter, we'll dive into the strategies and tactics you can use to make PR work for you. Get ready to take your brand to new heights!

QUESTIONS FOR REFLECTION:

How Credible Is Your Brand?

Are you currently leveraging third-party endorsements to build credibility? If not, how can you start incorporating them into your PR strategy?

Who Is Your Ideal Audience?

Have you clearly identified the right audience for your brand? How can PR help you reach these people more effectively?

What Makes Your Brand Unique?

What differentiates you from your competitors? How can PR help you highlight and amplify these unique aspects of your brand?

Are You Ready for the Spotlight?

Consider your readiness to handle increased visibility and scrutiny. How would your brand handle a PR crisis? Do you have a plan in place?

How Do You Want to Be Known?

Think about the legacy you want to build. What steps can you take now to ensure your brand is recognised as a leader in your industry?

POINTS TO CONSIDER:

The Power of Social Proof:

Reflect upon how seeing others endorse or engage with a brand influences your own behaviour. How can you create that same effect for your brand?

Long-Term Vision:

PR is not just about immediate gains. Consider how your current PR efforts are contributing to your long-term brand growth and market position.

Employee Morale:

How can you use PR to not only build external trust but foster a sense of pride and belonging within your team?

Audience Engagement:

Think about the ways in which PR can help you better connect with your audience. What strategies could you implement to deepen these connections?

Building Relationships:

PR is all about relationships. Are you actively building and nurturing relationships with the media, influencers and other stakeholders in your industry?

These questions and points should help you start thinking more strategically about how PR can serve as a powerful tool in building and maintaining your personal brand.

4

BUILDING A PERSONAL BRAND - BRAND LIKE JESUS

When it comes to building a personal brand, you need a solid foundation that will stand the test of time. At the heart of this foundation is what I call the **Jesus Branding Trinity**: To date Jesus arguably has one of, if not the most famous legacy of anyone who ever lived.

There are 3 key elements that contributed heavily to the enduring success of Jesus' brand and branding requires to develop a legacy brand

A **Hook**, a **Look**, and a **Book**. Let's break this down:

1. THE HOOK

Your hook is what grabs attention. It's that memorable thing about you that makes people stop scrolling or put down their coffee mid-sip because they want to know more. Think of it as your unique selling point. What's your story? What's the one thing that makes you different from everyone else? At the heart of PR, remember, is **storytelling**. You've got to hook people with a story that not only gets attention but keeps it.

A solid hook is more than just a flashy headline; it's the beginning of a journey you're inviting your audience on. Whether it's your personal triumphs, your failures, or that unique perspective only you can offer, the hook is the starting point. But here's the kicker: the hook must provide value. It needs to be **WIN, WIN, WIN, WIN** – a win for the reader, a win for the publication, a win for the journalist, and finally, a win for you.

2. THE LOOK

Next is the **look**. Whether you imagine he had long blonde hair and blue eyes or feet of brass and hair of wool, I'm willing to bet you can close your eyes and see his image or silhouette clearly.

This is likely to be the same with icons such as Michael Jackson, Marilyn Monroe. A look so distinctive they cannot be mistaken for anyone else.

Think of this as your personal brand's visual and emotional identity. It's how you present yourself, how you make people feel when they engage with you. From your website to your social media feeds, your "look" should be cohesive and reflective of your core identity.

Now, here's the important bit: **identity impacts core beliefs**, and your core beliefs shape your behaviours. If your personal brand doesn't align with who you really are, you're going to struggle. Before embarking on your PR journey, you need to get the identity piece sorted. When your identity is authentic, it shapes your personal narrative in a way that resonates deeply with your audience. Don't try to be something you're not; it won't last, and PR is a **long game**. We're not interested in flash-in-the-pan overnight success—we want sustained visibility.

And let's be real: people can sense authenticity from a mile away. When you show up as yourself, it creates trust and lasting engagement. This leads us to the final piece of the trinity...

3. THE BOOK

Don't panic if you haven't written an actual book yet. In this context, the **book** represents your body of work. It's the expertise, knowledge and experiences you've amassed that position you as a thought leader in your field. Whether you've written books, blogs, white papers, or given talks at industry conferences, this is where you prove you've got substance to back up the hook and the look.

But even if you haven't published anything yet, that's okay. Think of your "book" as the story you've been writing every day with your actions. It's the track record of success, impact, or growth that you can point to and say, "This is why I'm worth listening to."

PR IS A LONG GAME: THE POWER OF STORYTELLING

Once you've nailed your hook, look, and book, it's time to embrace the fact that **PR is a long game**. You're not going to become an industry sensation overnight. At the heart of great PR is storytelling, and stories take time to develop, unfold, and resonate. You have to be willing to commit to a sustained effort—consistent messaging, continuous value, and building relationships with journalists and publications.

If you're going to play the long game, you have to pace yourself. Which brings us to the concept of **Thunder and Lightning**.

THUNDER AND LIGHTNING: EMBRACE CAUSE AND EFFECT

Just as thunder follows lightning, for every action you take outside your comfort zone, there's a reaction. Think of it like this: Lightning is the bold move you make when you step out as a thought leader or push your brand into new territory. It's the initial spark of energy that creates visibility. But after that, you need time for **thunder**—the process of regulating, settling into your new space, and allowing the world to respond to your action.

In PR, every big splash requires a follow-up. After a major media feature or viral moment, give yourself space to regulate your nervous system, process the reactions, and maintain momentum without burning out.

MAIN CHARACTER ENERGY

One of the key ingredients in a successful personal brand is **Main Character Energy**. In your own story, you have to be the hero, not the supporting character. Too often, we treat ourselves like NPCs (non-player characters) in our own game. To be truly successful, you have to step into the role of the main character. You must embody the confidence, vision, and self-awareness that make people want to pay attention to you.

Being the main character doesn't mean being arrogant or self-centred. It means recognising your value, embracing your power, and showing up fully. The world is waiting for you to take up space, so stop holding back.

THE WIN, WIN, WIN, WIN FORMULA

Any story you pitch should be a **win for everyone involved**. If it's only beneficial to you, the pitch will fall flat. A successful PR story has to resonate with the **reader, publication**, **journalist**, and of course, **you** as the subject. If all four parties don't win, it's not a good pitch.

For the reader, the story has to provide value—whether it's entertainment, education, or inspiration. For the publication, it has to fit their brand and audience. For the journalist, it needs to be a compelling story that's worth telling. And for you, it needs to showcase your personal brand and serve your long-term goals.

By mastering the **Jesus Branding Trinity** and approaching PR with authenticity, patience, and strategy, you'll build a personal brand that not only stands out but also stands the test of time. Just remember: PR is a long game, but when played well, it's the most rewarding game in town.

5

THE AAA FAME PR FRAMEWORK

YOUR BLUEPRINT FOR PR SUCCESS

Hopefully by now, you've decided you're ready to conquer the world of PR? Well, buckle up because you're about to embark on a journey through the magical land of my very own **AAA PR Framework**. Trust me, this isn't your ordinary, stuffy PR guide; this is your blueprint to becoming a PR rockstar, the person everyone calls when they need to know how to get noticed, get loved and get ahead.

In this chapter, we're going to break down the AAA PR Framework, sprinkle in some benefits (because who doesn't love benefits?) and give you a step-by-step guide to getting started.

Before we start, I'd like to share the inspiration behind it. PR has traditionally been an area that cannot be directly linked to sales or revenue because of something called multi-touch attribution.

Multi-touch attribution recognises that a customer's decision to engage with a brand is influenced by multiple interactions across different channels, making it challenging to pinpoint a single touchpoint as the sole driver of conversion.

PR ROI and KPIs aren't as straightforward as those for marketing, largely because of the complexities of multi-touch attribution. In marketing, it's often easier to track a direct line from a campaign to a conversion, but PR operates in a more nuanced space. It involves numerous touchpoints – media mentions, social endorsements, word of mouth – that collectively build a brand's reputation over time. This makes it difficult to measure the immediate impact of PR efforts in simple metrics. However, the main reason most people invest in PR is the expectation that these efforts will increase revenue in the long term.

Recognising this, I developed the framework as an attempt to bridge the gap between the intangible nature of PR and the understandable desire of clients to have more certainty about the results they could expect, even if they couldn't be guaranteed. My method centres on the income, influence and impact trifecta, rooted in the understanding that generating income creates the foundation for influence, and with influence comes the ability to make a significant impact. The more income and influence one has, the greater the potential for impact. Instead of viewing money and fame as separate entities, I realised that they are two sides of the same coin. Both are necessary to create lasting change and meaningful success. This approach allows clients to see PR not just as a means to gain visibility but as a strategic tool to drive both financial and societal gains.

BRENDA GABRIEL PR

Fame PR Impact Pyramid

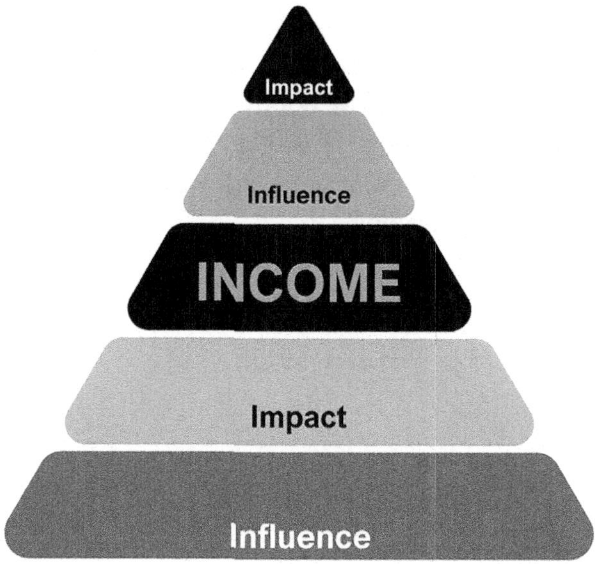

© 2023 Brenda Gabriel

THE AAA FAME PR FRAMEWORK

The AAA PR Framework is based on what I refer to as the holy trinity of public relations. It splits your PR activity into three distinct layers:

1. **Ascendance**: This is where you lay down the foundation. Think of it as building a house. Without a solid foundation, you're just one strong wind away from disaster. Here, we focus on getting your basics right: your purpose, your persona and your process.

2. **Affluence**: Now that your foundation is solid, it's time to move onto the fancy stuff: strategic positioning, growth and making sure your PR efforts don't just work, but work for *you*. This is where you start building that empire.
3. **Advancement**: Finally, we're talking about taking over the world. Okay, maybe not the whole world, but at least your corner of it. This pillar is all about scaling up, spreading your influence far and wide and becoming the name on everyone's lips.

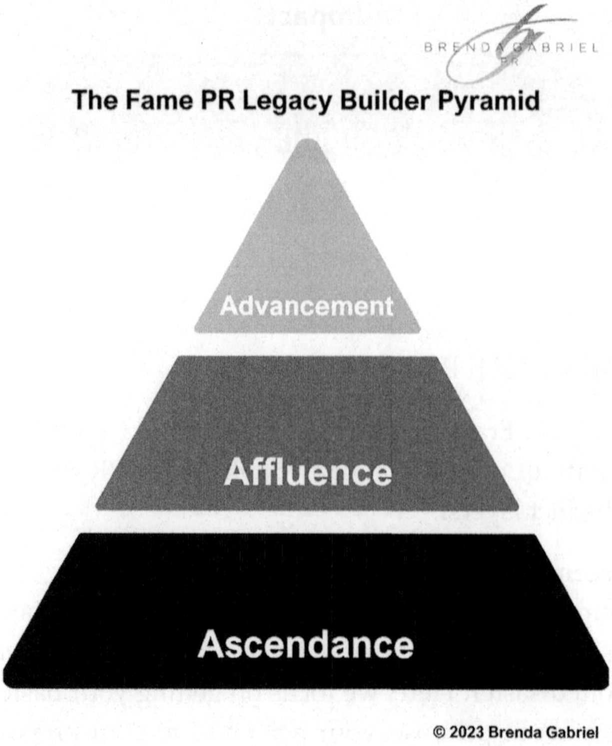

THE AAA FAME PR PYRAMID: UNPACKING THE MAGIC

1. Ascendance

   Laying the groundwork, leveraging PR and mass media communications to attain the level of influence required to get you from big vision to global prominence and massive impact.

Purpose: Why are you doing this? No, seriously, what's your big 'why'? Before you can be a PR superstar, you need to figure out what drives you. It is like the caffeine shot to your PR strategy. Without it, you're just going through the motions. Your purpose comes in three parts, which I like to call your 'BPL'. This acronym stands for business, personal and legacy.

Preparation: Like the Scouts always say, be prepared. Whether you're crafting a media pitch or planning a big event, preparation is your best friend. Otherwise, you might end up like that guy who showed up to the meeting in his pyjamas (awkward).

Perception: Ever heard the phrase, "Fake it till you make it"? Well, perception is reality in PR. You need to decide how you want the world to see you. Think of it as choosing your own superhero persona, cape optional but highly recommended.

Process: PR isn't just a one-hit wonder; it is more like a never-ending concert tour. You need a solid process to keep the hits coming. That means planning, executing and, of course, making sure everything runs smoothly.

Public Persona: This is the face you show to the world. It is your public persona, your brand, your 'I woke up like this' look. Whether you're going for polished professionalism or quirky charm, make sure it's consistent.

Parasocial Relationships: A fancy way of saying you want people to feel like they know you even if they've never met you. Think of it like being the cool kid in school who everyone wants to hang out with, even if they've only seen you in the hallway.

Personal Brand: Your personal brand is like your PR alter ego. It is all about what makes *you* unique. Are you the go-to expert on obscure facts? The life of the party? Whatever it is, own it.

Paradox: Here is where things get fun. Embrace the paradoxes. Be consistent but adaptable. Be innovative but reliable. It is like trying to be both Batman and Bruce Wayne at the same time: challenging but oh so worth it.

Principles: Last but not least, don't lose sight of your principles. They are your North Star, guiding you through the chaos of PR life. Stick to them and you'll always find your way home.

2. <u>Affluence</u>

Getting your house in order to increase surplus income that can be used to implement and deliver on your big vision.

Positioning: Where do you fit in the grand scheme of things? Positioning is all about staking your claim. Are you the best? The brightest? The most innovative? Find your niche and own it.

Proprietary Methodology: Fancy term alert! This just means you need your own secret sauce. What is your unique approach that sets you apart from the rest? Once you figure it out, bottle it up and sprinkle it everywhere.

Product Suite: Your PR efforts should show off your products or services in the best light. Imagine your product suite as the star of the show with your PR strategy as the spotlight. Shine that light bright!

Performance Indicators: It is all fun and games until someone asks for the numbers. Performance indicators are how you prove your PR is working. Think of them as the scoreboard that tells you whether you're winning or losing.

Pipeline: A strong pipeline is like having a VIP list for your PR party. It is your contacts, your media friends, your influencers: anyone who can help get your message out there. Keep that list updated and treat them like gold.

Proximity: How close are you to your audience? No, not in a creepy way. Proximity is all about making sure your message hits close to home. Know your audience and tailor your message to them.

Pre-eminence: Aim to be the go-to source in your field. When people think of your industry, they should think of you first. It is like being the top search result on Google but in real life.

3. <u>Advancement</u>

Building towards global and societal impact through cultural agency, crafting legacy and the evolution of society as a whole.

Purpose (Revisited): Your purpose might evolve as you grow. Check in with it from time to time like an old friend who gives great advice. Make sure it still fits where you're headed.

Platform/Publication: Own your platform. Whether it's a blog, a podcast or a YouTube channel, make it your domain. This is your soapbox; use it wisely.

Prospects: Keep the new leads coming! Always be on the lookout for fresh faces who might be interested in what you have to offer. Think of it like a never-ending networking event, minus the awkward small talk.

Patrons: These are your VIPs: the people who believe in you and your brand. Cultivate those relationships because they're the ones who will shout your praises from the rooftops.

Publicity: Publicity is like oxygen for your PR strategy. Without it, things will suffocate. Keep generating buzz, getting featured and staying in the public eye.

Prominence: As your influence grows, so should your prominence. You want to be the name on everyone's lips, the expert everyone calls when they need insight. Aim high!

Political Clout: Finally, don't underestimate the power of relationships in high places. Whether it's networking with industry leaders or getting in good with local influencers, having political clout can help you navigate tricky waters.

WHY THE AAA PROCESS WORKS

This process is designed to be comprehensive, ensuring that PR activity doesn't become a silo that has no link to other assets of business. Here are some of the benefits:

- Holistic Approach: No stone left unturned here. We cover it all, from PR to operational and financial considerations.
- Scalability: Whether you're a PR newbie or a seasoned pro, the AAA PR framework grows with you. There's always more that can be done in every layer.
- Strategic Alignment: Everything you do in PR will tie back to your business goals. No wasted effort, just results that matter.
- Increased Influence: People will go from, "Who's that?" to, "We need them on our panel ASAP!" Influence is your new best friend.
- Sustainability: PR is a marathon, not a sprint. The AAA PR framework ensures you're in it for the long haul.

GETTING STARTED: LET'S DO THIS!

Ready to get the PR party started? Here is your roadmap:

1. **Self-Assessment time**: Start by taking a good, hard look in the mirror. Where do you stand in each of the three areas? Be honest as this is where you figure out what's working and what's, well, not.
2. **Goal Setting**: What do you want out of this? More brand awareness? Industry domination? Whatever it is, set clear, specific goals. It is like choosing your destination before hitting the road.

3. **Strategy Development**: Now that you know where you want to go, map out your route. Your PR strategy should cover all the bases: ascendance, affluence and advancement. It is like building your dream team: make sure every position is covered.
4. **Implementation**: Time to put that plan into action! Start pitching, posting and promoting like your life depends on it (Well, maybe not your life, but definitely your career).
5. **Monitor and Adjust**: PR is a living, breathing thing. Keep an eye on how things are going, track those KPIs and be ready to tweak your strategy as needed. It is like tending to a garden: nurture it and it will grow.

CONCLUSION

The AAA PR framework isn't just a guide; it is your new best friend in the PR world. By focusing on ascendance, affluence and advancement, you'll build a strategy that not only works, but works wonders. So grab your cape, put on your PR superhero suit and get ready to take your influence, income and impact to the next level.

Now, let's go out there and show the world what you've got!

6

ARE YOU READY FOR PR?

This is a question I've been asked numerous times. It shines a light on the widespread confusion over the purpose of PR, how it works and the advantages of actively engaging in it for, well, *you*.

So how do you know if you're ready for PR?

Spoiler alert: you are already doing it.

Public relations at its core is *managing* how people perceive and feel about you, your business or your brand. The biggest misconception about PR is the belief that it's something you can opt out off when we're always managing the way we're seen by others.

Landing a single article in a newspaper doesn't make you ready for PR; neither does hiring a PR agency. If you're talking 'shop' on your personal profile, congratulations! You are engaging in personal brand PR. The real question isn't how you know if you're ready for PR; it is whether you're curating or just rolling the dice on public perception. PR readiness isn't just about having a flashy brand or a hefty budget (though both certainly help); it is about a deep, honest assessment of where you are, what you want to achieve and whether you're truly prepared to dive into the world of public relations. Spoiler alert: this isn't for the faint of heart or those looking for instant gratification. It requires self-awareness, commitment and a fair amount of grit. Let's break down what you need to consider before embarking on your PR journey.

SELF-AWARENESS AND REALISTIC EXPECTATIONS

PR is not a magic wand. You can't just wave it and expect overnight fame, viral posts or an instant surge in sales. It's a strategic, long-term effort that demands patience and a clear understanding of what you want to achieve. Are you looking to build brand awareness, establish thought leadership or perhaps secure investment? Whatever your goals, it's crucial to set realistic expectations from the outset.

If you're dreaming of being featured on *Good Morning America* next week or expect that one press release will make you the next industry superstar, it's time for a reality check. PR takes time, and its effects are often cumulative. You need to be in it for the long haul, ideally with a budget that supports sustained activity over six to twelve months and beyond.

Remember, even if you're not actively investing in PR right now, you are still engaging in it. Every encounter someone has with your brand, every review – good or bad – every word-of-mouth recommendation is PR. Your public image is always being shaped, whether you're consciously steering it or not.

In essence, the question isn't if you are ready for PR; it is what stage of the PR process you are at.

What level of resourcing do you have available to invest in PR? Do you know enough about it to make an informed decision about your PR strategy, whether you decide to keep it in-house or outsource it?

Embarking on a PR journey is not for the faint of heart. Public relations is an investment of time, money, energy and, most importantly, your reputation. PR can be incredibly powerful, but it requires a deep level of commitment and readiness. It is not something you should rush into without serious consideration. So, before you dive in, ask yourself: are you really ready for PR?

PR IS NOT A MAGIC WAND

First things first, PR is not a magic wand that will instantly catapult you into the spotlight. If you're looking for overnight results, you're setting yourself up for disappointment. Publicity takes time. Even the best publicists with their golden Rolodexes need a compelling story to tell. Relationships with editors, producers and journalists matter, but if your story isn't strong, it won't get picked up. PR is about building relationships and credibility over time, not about making quick headlines.

PR REQUIRES YOUR ACTIVE PARTICIPATION

One of the biggest misconceptions about PR is that it's something you can hand off to an expert and forget about. Sorry, but that's not how it works. Think of PR as a sport: you've got to be in the game, not just sitting on the sidelines. The clients who see the best results are the ones who are actively engaged in the process. They read the news, share stories with their publicist and respond promptly to opportunities. In short, they put in the work.

PR is a partnership. Your publicist can't manufacture thought leadership content out of thin air. They need your insights, your expertise and your unique perspective. If you're not willing or able to provide that, your PR efforts will fall flat.

PR IS NOT A DIRECT SALES TOOL

Let's clear up another common misconception: PR is not your sales team. The role of a publicist is to create stories that capture the media's attention, not to close deals. If you're expecting every piece of media coverage to translate directly into sales, you're going to be disappointed. The value of PR lies in the long-term visibility, credibility and brand recognition it builds, not in immediate sales spikes.

Think of PR as planting seeds. Some will take root and grow into something substantial, while others might not bear fruit right away. It is a long game, and if you're only in it for short-term gains, you're missing the bigger picture.

FAME IS NOT A STRATEGY

If your goal is simply to become famous, PR is not the answer. Fame for fame's sake is an empty pursuit. Instead, think about what you want to be known for. What's your story? What makes you unique? A good publicist can help you bring attention to what makes you special, but they can't make you special. Fame should be the byproduct of years of hard work, dedication and passion in your field, not the end goal.

YOU NEED A NEWSWORTHY STORY

Everyone thinks their new business, product or service is groundbreaking, but the reality is that the media sees countless pitches every day. What makes your story stand out? If you haven't thought through why the media should care, you're not ready for PR. It is your publicist's job to help craft the narrative, but they need substance to work with. Without a newsworthy angle, even the most skilled publicist will struggle to get you the coverage you're hoping for.

PR WON'T FIX BUSINESS PROBLEMS

PR is not a band-aid for underlying business issues. In fact, it can often shine a spotlight on them. If your company has high turnover, poor customer service or other internal problems, these issues are likely to surface once you start gaining media attention. It is better to have your house in order before inviting the world to take a closer look. PR can amplify your strengths, but it can also magnify your weaknesses.

DON'T CHASE YOUR COMPETITOR'S SUCCESS

Just because your competitor landed a spot on a major TV show doesn't mean you should be on TV too. PR should be about what's right for your brand, not about *Keeping Up with the Joneses*. If you're not prepared to drop everything for a press hit or if your business can't handle the attention, then chasing media coverage might do more harm than good. PR should be a long-term commitment, not a reactionary move.

BE READY FOR THE LONG HAUL

PR is a marathon, not a sprint. It requires patience, persistence and a willingness to stay the course even when results aren't immediate. The most successful PR clients are those who understand the value of consistency and are willing to invest in a long-term relationship with their publicist. Changing agencies every few months because you're not seeing instant results will only set you back. Trust the process and give it time to work.

THE NEED FOR OPERATIONAL READINESS

Imagine this: your PR campaign kicks off and, suddenly, there's a surge of interest in your business. Your website traffic spikes, your phone won't stop ringing and your inbox is flooded with inquiries. Sounds like a dream, right? But here's the catch: if your business isn't operationally ready, this dream can quickly turn into a nightmare.

Operational readiness means having the capacity and systems in place to handle increased awareness and sales. It is about ensuring that your business can smoothly convert the interest generated by PR into actual revenue. This involves everything from having enough inventory to fulfil orders, to ensuring your website can handle increased traffic, to having a team ready to respond to inquiries promptly.

THE EMOTIONAL AND MENTAL TOLL OF PR

Finally, it's important to be mentally and emotionally prepared for the journey ahead. PR can put you in the public eye in ways you might not be prepared for. Increased visibility comes with increased scrutiny. Are you ready for that? Can you handle criticism or negative feedback? Are you prepared to put yourself out there, day after day, knowing that not everyone will like what you have to say?

PR isn't just about the good times; it is about weathering the storms. Having a strong support system in place, whether it's a mentor, a coach or a therapist, can make all the difference. Do not forget about the importance of self-care. The pressure of being in the spotlight can take a toll on your mental and emotional health, so it's crucial to take care of yourself throughout the process.

CONCLUSION

PR can be a game-changer for your business, but only if you're truly ready for it. It requires time, effort and a deep level of commitment. It's not a quick fix, nor a guarantee of instant success. But if you're willing to put in the work, stay the course and invest in the long-term, PR can help you build a brand that stands the test of time.

Before you take the plunge, take a moment to reflect upon whether you're really ready for PR. Do you have a newsworthy story? Are you prepared for the time and effort required? Is your business operationally ready to handle increased attention? Perhaps most importantly, are you mentally and emotionally prepared for the journey ahead?

If the answer is yes, then you're ready to embark on one of the most rewarding journeys you'll ever take, one that has the potential to transform not just your business but your life.

QUESTIONS TO ASK YOURSELF:

What are my specific PR goals?

Am I prepared for the long-term commitment that PR requires?

Do I have a budget that can sustain PR efforts for at least six to twelve months?

BUDGETING FOR PR

PR is an investment, not an expense, and like any investment, you need to approach it strategically. How much should you be spending? While there's no one-size-fits-all answer, a good rule of thumb is to allocate between 5 to 10% of your gross revenue to PR. But this will vary depending on your business stage, goals and industry competition.

Here are four strategies to consider when budgeting for media coverage:

1. Available Funds for PR in Budget: Look at what you can realistically allocate to PR after covering your essential expenses.
2. Percentage of Revenue: Allocate a set percentage of your revenue towards PR. This ensures that your PR investment grows as your business grows.
3. Based on Business and PR Goals: Tailor your budget to what you want to achieve. Launching a new product? You might need to spend more. Looking to maintain visibility? You could get away with spending less.
4. Based on Competitors' PR Strategies: Look at what your competitors are doing. Are they everywhere? Then you might need to up your game to keep pace.

KEEP IN MIND:

Advertising costs for luxury products are always higher than for essentials.

Launching a new product requires significant PR and marketing investment.

Niches with high competition often demand more aggressive PR spending.

QUESTIONS TO ASK YOURSELF:

What percentage of my revenue can I allocate to PR?

Are my competitors outspending me in PR, and how might that affect my market position?

What are the specific goals I want my PR budget to achieve?

7
PREPARING FOR PR: BUILDING A STRONG FOUNDATION

Stepping into the world of PR is a bold move, and like any big step, it requires some serious preparation. If preparing for a marathon, you wouldn't just throw on your trainers and hit the pavement without some training, right? In the same way, successful PR demands that you build a solid foundation emotionally, mentally, operationally and in terms of your brand's public-facing presence. So let's dive into what it takes to get truly ready for PR.

EMOTIONAL AND MENTAL PREPARATION: REGULATING YOUR NERVOUS SYSTEM

First things first, let's talk about your headspace. The journey of PR, especially one that leads to increased visibility and influence, can be a bit of an emotional rollercoaster. You are putting yourself out there, and that means facing scrutiny, criticism and, sometimes, a lot of noise. This is where emotional and mental preparation comes in.

In addition to regular stress management techniques, I would recommend working with a specialised expert in whichever area you might feel you require the most help. This could be a coach or therapist well versed in dealing with your specific challenges.

Nervous System Regulation: Your nervous system is the control centre for how you react to stress. When stepping into the public eye, the pressure can trigger your fight-or-flight response. To avoid feeling overwhelmed, it's crucial to develop strategies for regulating your nervous system.

I am a huge fan of therapeutic techniques including EMDR (eye movement desensitisation and reprocessing) or somatic therapy, which can help process underlying anxieties or traumas that might surface as you step into greater visibility.

I have even worked with a money specialist who works with celebrities and high-net-worth individuals (HNWIs) to take them back to the root of their money programming, which can have a major impact on their willingness to become more visible.

Being mentally and emotionally prepared is just as important as having the right PR strategy. When you feel strong and grounded, you're better equipped to handle whatever comes your way.

OPERATIONAL AND FUNCTIONAL READINESS: GETTING YOUR HOUSE IN ORDER

Let's move on to the operational side of things. Before you step into the spotlight, your backend operations need to be solid. After all, you don't want to attract attention only to drop the ball when it comes to delivering what you promise.

Operational Backend: Your business operations should be smooth and efficient. Make sure your systems, whether for customer service, order fulfilment or client communication, are ready to handle an influx of attention.

- **Automation Tools:** Consider investing in automation tools that can handle routine tasks so you can focus on the more strategic aspects of your PR campaign. CRM (Customer Relationship Management) systems, email marketing platforms and project management tools can all help keep things running smoothly.
- **Team Readiness:** Ensure your team is on the same page and prepared to support your PR efforts. This might involve training them on how to handle media inquiries, manage an uptick in customer interactions or ensure quality control as your visibility increases.
- **Scalability:** Can your business handle a sudden spike in demand? Make sure you have the infrastructure in place to scale quickly if needed, whether that's through flexible staffing solutions, additional inventory or streamlined processes.

People Support: Having the right people in your corner is crucial. Whether it's a PR agency, a personal assistant or a mentor, surround yourself with individuals who can offer expertise, guidance and support as you navigate this journey.

- **PR Team:** A good PR team will be your strategic partner, helping you craft your message, identify opportunities and manage any challenges that arise.
- **Mentors and Advisors:** Having mentors who have walked the path before you can provide invaluable insights and help you avoid common pitfalls.

BUILDING CREDIBILITY: THE BASICS OF BRAND READINESS

Now that you're emotionally, mentally and operationally prepared, let's focus on the public-facing side of things. Before you can successfully engage in PR, you need to ensure your brand is ready to be showcased to the world.

Build Credibility: Credibility is the bedrock of effective PR. If people are going to trust you, they need to see that you're the real deal. Here is how you can build that credibility:

- **Testimonials and Reviews:** Collect testimonials from past clients or customers and showcase them on your website and social media platforms. Positive reviews serve as social proof that you deliver on your promises.
- **Case Studies:** If you have successful projects or clients you've worked with, create detailed case studies that highlight your impact. These can be powerful tools for demonstrating your expertise.
- **Awards and Recognition:** If you've received any awards or industry recognition, make sure they're prominently displayed. These accolades help position you as a leader in your field.

Media Kit: A media kit is your PR toolkit. It should include all the essential information about you and your brand that a journalist or media outlet might need:

- **Bio:** A well-crafted biography that highlights your achievements, expertise and unique selling points.
- **Professional Headshots:** High-quality images that the media can use in their coverage.
- **Press Releases:** Any recent press releases or newsworthy updates.
- **Case Studies and Testimonials:** A selection of your most impactful case studies and testimonials.
- **Contact Information:** Make it easy for the media to get in touch with you.

Website and Corporate Messaging: Your website is often the first place people will go to learn more about you. Make sure it's polished, professional and reflects your brand's values and mission.

Clear Messaging: Your website should clearly communicate who you are, what you do and why it matters. Ensure your messaging is consistent across all platforms.

SEO Optimisation: Make sure your website is optimised for search engines so that people can easily find you.

Blog and Content: Regularly updated content, such as a blog or news section, can help establish you as a thought leader in your industry.

CORE STORY EXERCISE: CRAFTING YOUR NARRATIVE

Finally, to truly stand out in the crowded media landscape, you need a compelling core story: a narrative that captures who you are, what you stand for and why people should care.

The Core Story Exercise: Your core story is the heart of your brand. It is the narrative that will guide all of your PR efforts, from media interviews to social media posts. To craft it, ask yourself the following questions:

What is your origin story? How did you get to where you are today? What challenges have you overcome?

What drives you? What are your values and mission? What impact do you want to make in the world?

Why should people care? What makes your story unique? How does it resonate with your target audience?

Once you've answered these questions, distil your answers into a clear, concise narrative. This core story will serve as the foundation for all your PR efforts.

As a thank you for purchasing this book, I'm offering a free, in-depth core story exercise worksheet to help you craft your narrative. Email us at: support@brendagabriel.co.uk *and we'll send it across.*

READY, SET, GO!

By now, you should have a clear understanding of what it takes to prepare for a successful PR journey. From getting your emotional and mental game strong to ensuring your operations are smooth and your brand is credible, you're laying the groundwork for impactful visibility. Remember, PR is not just about getting attention; it is about making sure you're ready to handle that attention when it comes.

As you embark on this journey, keep in mind that preparation is key. The more solid your foundation, the more successful your PR efforts will be. So take the time to get everything in place, and then get ready to shine.

8
WHAT TO LOOK FOR IN A PR AGENCY

COMMON PR PITFALLS

If you're new to the world of PR, navigating the landscape of public relations agencies can feel like wandering through a maze in the dark. You know you need PR, but what exactly should you be looking for? The truth is that most people don't know what to look for in a PR agency, and that's not their fault. PR can be a complex field and unless you've worked in the industry, you're likely unfamiliar with the intricacies involved.

I have lost count of the horror stories I've heard from clients who came to me after bad experiences with other agencies. There is the tale of the entrepreneur who spent nine months with an expensive PR agency, only to walk away without a single piece of coverage. When I took over, I secured over one hundred pieces within twelve months, including a feature in the first week. Then there's the tech startup founder who trusted a budget agency to tell their story, only to find themselves plastered across tabloids in a less-than-flattering light. Instead of focusing on how their innovation could change lives, the agency went for cheap sensationalism.

Don't get me started on the agency that agreed to secure paid speaking gigs for a client, failed miserably and then neglected to suggest any improvements that could have increased the client's chances of success, or the cheap agency that, after failing to secure coverage during a short-term contract, offered a month of free PR as a consolation then ghosted the client entirely.

I seem to be the one people find when things have gone wrong elsewhere. I'm the PR agency they call when other agencies aren't hitting it right. But instead of focusing on those negative experiences, let's talk about how to avoid them in the first place. Here is a guide on what to look for in a PR agency to make sure you're getting the right partner for your business.

1. Passion for You and Your Business

First and foremost, your PR agency should be genuinely excited about you and your business. PR is about telling your story, and if your agency doesn't care about your story, how can they possibly tell it well? Passion isn't just nice to have; it is essential. If your PR team isn't invested in your success, they're not going to go the extra mile for you.

For me, I'm very selective about who I take on as clients. I only work with people I genuinely connect with: people I could see myself going on holiday with. This isn't just about having a good time; it is about chemistry and shared values.

When I'm passionate about a client's mission, it drives me to deliver results that are above and beyond what's expected. So find an agency that's as passionate about your business as you are.

2. A Clear Roadmap to Success

A good PR agency should be able to provide you with a clear roadmap showing how they plan to get you from where you are now to where you want to be. This is more than just a list of services; they should have a strategic plan tailored to your specific needs and goals.

At my agency, we use the AAA Fame PR Pyramid, a clear visual representation of the journey to impactful fame. It outlines the steps we'll take together, from building your brand foundation to achieving your highest aspirations. If an agency can't show you a roadmap, that's a red flag. You need to know they have a plan and that they know how to execute it.

3. Industry Knowledge or the Willingness to Learn Quickly

While it's beneficial if a PR agency has experience in your specific industry, what's more important is their ability to learn quickly and ask the right questions. The best PR results come from going deep, and that means the agency needs to understand your business at a fundamental level.

I am often told that I ask questions my clients have never been asked before. That is because I dive deep to uncover the essence of what makes their business unique. A great PR agency will do the same: they will dig into your story, your challenges and your goals, and they'll use that information to craft a PR strategy that's as effective as it is authentic.

4. Alignment with Your Business Goals

PR isn't just about getting media coverage; it is about achieving your overarching business goals. A great PR agency will always link their work back to your broader objectives. Whether you're looking to increase brand awareness, drive sales or position yourself as a thought leader, your PR strategy should be aligned with these goals.

At my agency, we don't just pitch stories; we strategise with our clients to ensure that every piece of PR we secure is moving them closer to their business objectives. If an agency can't explain how their work will help you achieve your goals, that's a major red flag.

5. Experience in Securing the Right Media Exposure

Not all media exposure is created equal. The type of media coverage you need depends on your industry, your audience and your goals. A good PR agency should have experience securing the type of coverage that's right for you.

They should have a clear idea of the angles that will work for you and the outlets that are most likely to be interested in your story. They should also be able to explain why these angles and outlets are the best fit for your goals. If they can't, they might not have the experience you need.

6. Honesty and Expectation Management

PR is a long game, and anyone who promises you overnight results is selling you snake oil. A good PR agency will be honest with you about what's achievable based on your budget and timescales. They will manage your expectations and keep you informed every step of the way.

I always make it a point to be upfront with my clients about what's possible within their budget and timeframe. PR isn't cheap, but it shouldn't be something you scrimp on. Reputation is everything, and it's worth investing in an agency that will protect and enhance yours.

7. Proven Track Record of Success

When evaluating a PR agency, look for evidence of their past successes. This could be in the form of case studies, testimonials or even awards. A solid track record shows that they have a history of delivering results. Ask for specific examples of campaigns they've run that are similar to what you're looking for. Success in one industry doesn't always translate to another, so make sure they've got experience that's relevant to your needs.

8. Strong Media Relationships

The best PR agencies have strong, established relationships with journalists, editors, influencers and media outlets. These relationships are crucial because they can make the difference between a pitch that gets picked up and one that gets ignored. Do not be shy about asking the agency how they've leveraged their media relationships in the past. A good agency will have no problem providing examples of how their connections have benefitted their clients.

9. Creative Thinking and Innovation

PR is as much about creativity as it is about strategy. You want an agency that isn't afraid to think outside the box and come up with innovative ideas that will set you apart from the competition. Whether it's a unique campaign angle, a viral social media strategy or a clever publicity stunt, creativity is key to cutting through the noise. Ask potential agencies how they've approached challenges in the past and how they plan to bring fresh ideas to your PR efforts.

10. Transparency and Communication

Good communication is essential in any relationship, and that includes the one you have with your PR agency. You should expect regular updates on what's happening with your campaign, including what's working, what's not and what adjustments are being made. Look for an agency that is transparent about their processes, timelines and fees. You want to feel like a partner in the process, not just a client who gets billed at the end of the month.

11. Flexibility and Adaptability

The world of PR is constantly changing: what worked yesterday might not work tomorrow. That is why it's important to choose an agency that is flexible and adaptable. They should be able to pivot quickly when necessary, whether that's due to changes in the media landscape, shifts in your business goals or unexpected crises. Ask them about a time when they had to adapt on the fly and how they handled it.

12. A Comprehensive Approach

An effective PR strategy doesn't rely on just one tactic; it is a multi-faceted approach that includes media relations, content creation, social media, event planning and more. The agency you choose should have expertise in all of these areas and be able to integrate them into a cohesive strategy. The PESO model (paid, earned, shared and owned media) is a good framework for this. Make sure the agency can explain how they'll use a mix of these elements to achieve your goals.

13. Crisis Management Expertise

Every business faces challenges, and how you handle them can make or break your reputation. A good PR agency should have a solid crisis management plan in place and be able to guide you through any PR disasters that might come your way. This includes having a proactive approach to identifying potential issues before they become full-blown crises. Ask the agency how they've handled crises in the past and what their approach would be if something went wrong with your campaign.

14. Long-Term Vision

PR isn't just about the quick win; it is about building a lasting reputation. Your PR agency should have a long-term vision for your brand and be committed to helping you achieve sustained success. This means looking beyond the immediate campaign and thinking about how your brand will evolve over time. Discuss with the agency how they see your brand's future and how they plan to help you get there.

15. Client-Centric Approach

Finally, a great PR agency should put you at the centre of everything they do. They should take the time to understand your business, your goals and your values and tailor their approach to fit your unique needs. You want an agency that is as committed to your success as you are. Look for an agency that listens to your input, respects your feedback and is dedicated to making your vision a reality.

DO NOT GO FOR THE CHEAPEST OPTION

I get it: everyone loves a bargain. But when it comes to PR, you get what you pay for. The uninitiated often go for the cheapest option, only to end up disappointed. PR is an investment in your reputation, your brand and your future success. It is not something to cut corners on.

Think of PR as a partnership, not a one-off transaction. You are not just hiring an agency; you are bringing on a team that will represent you to the world. Make sure they're the right team.

WRAPPING UP: FINDING THE RIGHT FIT

Choosing the right PR agency is a big decision, and it's one that shouldn't be taken lightly. By looking for an agency that is passionate, strategic, creative, transparent and adaptable, you'll be setting yourself up for success. Remember, your PR agency is an extension of your brand, and their work will reflect upon you. Take the time to find a partner who not only understands your goals but is committed to helping you achieve them in the most effective and impactful way possible.

9

ADDRESSING COMMON PR FEARS

When it comes to public relations, there's no shortage of excitement and anticipation. But let's be real, there's also a healthy dose of fear. Why wouldn't there be? You are putting your brand, your message and, in many cases, your personal reputation out there for the world to see. It is only natural to have a few jitters. In this chapter, we'll explore some of the most common fears that clients face when they embark on a PR journey, how strategic PR can help address these fears and how to build influence and authority both internally and externally.

Let's start by diving into the big three: message dilution, narrative control and public perception. These are the nightmares that keep even the most seasoned business owners awake at night.

COMMON FEARS

1. MESSAGE DILUTION

- **The Fear:** You have spent countless hours crafting your message. It is sharp, it's clear and it's everything you want your brand to be. But what if it gets watered down? What if the core of your message gets lost in translation or, worse, misinterpreted?
- **The Reality:** This fear is entirely valid. In a world where information moves at lightning speed, it's easy for a message to get diluted as it passes through different channels. The last thing you want is for your message to be so vague that it fails to resonate or, on the flip side, so complex that it confuses your audience.

2. NARRATIVE CONTROL

- **The Fear:** You are the one who knows your brand best, so naturally, you want to control the story that gets told. But the moment you hand your story over to the media, you lose a bit of that control. What if a journalist takes your words out of context? What if your message is twisted into something you never intended?
- **The Reality:** Losing control of the narrative is a genuine concern. Once your story is out in the public domain, it's open to interpretation. The challenge is to guide the narrative as much as possible while being prepared to respond if things take an unexpected turn.

3. PUBLIC PERCEPTION

- **The Fear:** Public perception is a powerful thing. One misstep, one poorly chosen word, and suddenly your brand is under fire. You worry about how people will perceive you, your company and your message. Will they love it, or will they pick it apart?
- **The Reality:** Public perception can indeed make or break a brand. In today's world, where everyone has an opinion and a platform to voice it, public perception is more crucial than ever. This fear underscores the importance of crafting a message that resonates with your audience and aligns with your brand values.

HOW STRATEGIC PR ADDRESSES THESE FEARS AND SUPPORTS YOUR GOALS

Now that we've laid out the fears, let's talk about how PR can help you overcome them and support your goals.

1. STRATEGIC MESSAGING TO COMBAT MESSAGE DILUTION

- **How PR Helps:** One of the core functions of PR is to help you craft a message that's not just strong but consistent across all channels. A good PR strategy involves developing key messages that can be adapted to different platforms without losing their essence. This ensures that whether your audience hears your message on TV, reads it in a blog or sees it on social media, the core of your message remains intact.

2. MEDIA TRAINING AND PREPARATION TO MAINTAIN NARRATIVE CONTROL

   - **How PR Helps:** While you can't control how a journalist will interpret your story, you can control how well prepared you are. Media training is a crucial part of PR, helping you to deliver your message clearly, handle tough questions and stay on point during interviews. The more prepared you are, the more control you'll have over how your story is told.

3. BUILDING A POSITIVE PUBLIC PERCEPTION THROUGH CONSISTENCY AND TRANSPARENCY

   - **How PR Helps:** Consistency and transparency are key to building a positive public perception. PR helps by ensuring that your messaging aligns with your brand values and is delivered consistently across all platforms. Additionally, PR professionals are skilled in crisis management, so if things do go south, they can help you navigate the situation and maintain public trust.

BUILDING INFLUENCE AND AUTHORITY: INTERNALLY AND EXTERNALLY

Beyond addressing fears, PR plays a pivotal role in building your influence and authority both within your organisation and the public sphere.

1. INTERNAL INFLUENCE AND AUTHORITY

- **Why it Matters:** Building influence internally is just as important as external recognition. When your team believes in the brand and its message, they become your biggest advocates. Internal PR focuses on fostering a strong company culture, ensuring that everyone, from the CEO to the newest hire, understands and supports the brand's mission.
- **How PR Helps:** Effective internal communication strategies, such as regular updates, transparent leadership and employee engagement initiatives, help to build this internal authority. When your team is on board, they are more likely to champion the brand externally, creating a ripple effect that amplifies your PR efforts.

2. EXTERNAL INFLUENCE AND AUTHORITY

- **Why it Matters:** External authority is about being seen as a leader in your industry. This not only helps to attract customers but positions you as a go-to expert, opening doors to new opportunities such as speaking engagements, partnerships and media coverage.

- **How PR Helps:** PR helps build external authority through thought leadership, media placements and strategic partnerships. By consistently sharing your expertise and insights in the right forums, you establish yourself as an authority in your field. This external recognition can lead to increased trust, credibility and, ultimately, business growth.

CONCLUSION

PR is a powerful tool for overcoming fears and achieving your goals. By addressing concerns like message dilution, narrative control and public perception head-on and by building influence and authority both internally and externally, PR sets the stage for lasting success. Remember, while the fears are real, they can be managed with the right strategy, preparation and support. The key is to approach PR as a long-term investment in your brand's reputation and influence rather than a quick fix. When done right, PR doesn't just mitigate risks; it turns them into opportunities for growth and success.

10
MEASURING SUCCESS

So you've launched your PR campaign and you're eager to see if it's making waves. But how do you measure success in PR? Unlike paid advertising, where you can directly track clicks and conversions, PR is more about shaping perceptions and building relationships, which can make success feel a bit harder to pin down. But don't worry, that's what this chapter is all about: understanding the key performance indicators (KPIs) that matter and how to evaluate the impact of your PR efforts.

UNDERSTANDING KEY PERFORMANCE INDICATORS (KPIS) FOR PR

KPIs are the metrics that help you gauge whether your PR efforts are hitting the mark. They are like the scorecard for your campaign, telling you what's working, what needs tweaking and what's missing the mark entirely. Let's break down the essential KPIs for PR:

1. Awareness

What it Is: Awareness is all about how many people know about your brand, product or campaign. It is the first step in the customer journey and a fundamental goal of any PR strategy.

How to Measure: Look at metrics like media reach (how many people have the potential to see your coverage), impressions (the number of times your content is displayed) and search engine traffic. Tools like Google Analytics, Mention and media monitoring software can help track these metrics.

2. Brand Mentions

What it Is: Brand mentions refer to how often your brand is mentioned across media channels, whether that's in the news, blogs, social media or podcasts.

How to Measure: Use media monitoring tools like Meltwater, Brandwatch or Mention to track how frequently and where your brand is being mentioned. Pay attention not just to the quantity but to the quality of these mentions: are they positive, neutral or negative?

3. Media Engagement

What it Is: Media engagement goes beyond just getting your brand mentioned; it is about how media outlets, journalists and bloggers are interacting with your story.

How to Measure: Track the depth of coverage: did the outlet just mention you in passing or did they feature an in-depth article? Also, consider the authority and relevance of the media outlet to your target audience. High engagement might mean a well-placed feature in a top-tier publication rather than just a blurb in a less influential one.

4. Social Media Metrics

What it Is: Social media metrics gauge how your campaign is performing across platforms like Twitter, Instagram, Facebook, LinkedIn and TikTok.

How to Measure: Track likes, shares, comments, retweets and mentions. Pay close attention to engagement rates, which give you a better sense of how your audience is interacting with your content. Use tools like Hootsuite, Sprout Social or native platform analytics to gather data.

5. Share of Voice (SOV)

What it Is: Share of voice measures how much of the conversation your brand owns compared to your competitors.

How to Measure: SOV is typically calculated as a percentage of total media mentions in your industry or category. If you have twenty mentions and your competitors have eighty combined, your SOV would be 20%. Tools like Meltwater or Talkwalker can help calculate SOV.

6. Sentiment Analysis

What it Is: Sentiment analysis examines the tone of the mentions and coverage your brand is receiving. Are people talking about you in a positive, neutral or negative light?

How to Measure: Media monitoring tools often include sentiment analysis features that assess the emotional tone of text. You can manually review mentions for context, but automated tools help when dealing with large volumes of data.

7. Website Traffic

What it Is: Website traffic measures how many people are visiting your site as a result of your PR efforts.

How to Measure: Use Google Analytics to track increases in traffic during your campaign, paying attention to referral sources. If your PR campaign includes backlinks, check to see how much traffic they're driving to your site.

8. Lead Generation and Conversions

What it Is: In some cases, PR can be directly linked to lead generation and conversions, especially in B2B campaigns or when offering downloadable resources.

How to Measure: Track how many leads or sales are generated from PR-driven traffic using tools like Google Analytics or your CRM system. Look for spikes in conversions during the campaign period.

9. Audience Engagement

What it Is: This is about how your target audience is interacting with your brand's content across all channels, including social media, email and your website.

How to Measure: Monitor metrics like time spent on page, bounce rate and click-through rates. Tools like Google Analytics and social media platforms' native insights will provide this data.

EVALUATING AND REVIEWING PR CAMPAIGNS

Once your campaign is up and running, or once it's completed, it's time to dive into evaluation. Here is how you can go about reviewing your PR campaign:

1. Compare Against Goals

Start by revisiting the SMART goals you set at the beginning of your campaign. Did you achieve what you set out to do? For example, if your goal was to increase brand awareness by 20%, how close did you get to that target?

2. Analyse the Data

Gather all your KPIs and look at the data holistically. Which channels performed the best? Where did you see the most engagement? Did any particular piece of content outperform the others?

3. Assess the Quality of Coverage

Quality matters just as much as quantity. Review the type of coverage you received: was it positive and aligned with your core messaging? Did you secure placements in high-authority outlets that reach your target audience?

4. Understand the Impact

Take the time to assess the broader impact of your campaign. Did it change the conversation around your brand? Did it open doors to new opportunities, such as speaking engagements, partnerships or new customer segments?

5. Identify Lessons Learned

No campaign is perfect, but there's always room for improvement. Identify what worked well and what didn't. Were there any missed opportunities or unexpected challenges? Use these insights to refine your approach for future campaigns.

6. Gather Stakeholder Feedback

If you're working with a team or agency, gather feedback from all stakeholders. This might include input from your PR agency, in-house marketing team, sales team or even customers. Understanding different perspectives can provide valuable insights.

7. Report and Communicate Results

Create a comprehensive report that summarises your findings. This should include an overview of the campaign, the goals, the outcomes and the recommendations for future efforts. Share this with key stakeholders to ensure everyone is aligned on the results and next steps.

8. Iterate and Plan Forward

Based on your evaluation, start planning your next move. What are the next steps to capitalising on the momentum generated by the campaign? Whether it's a follow-up campaign, a new product launch or a brand repositioning, use the lessons learned to inform your strategy moving forward.

CASE STUDIES: REAL-WORLD PR SUCCESS

To bring these principles to life, let's take a look at a couple of real-world examples where strategic measurement led to PR success:

CASE STUDY 1: APPLE'S IPHONE LAUNCHES

Apple is a master of PR, and their iPhone launches are a textbook example of how to measure success. Apple sets clear goals for their launches: building hype, driving pre-orders and generating media buzz. By tracking media mentions, social media engagement and pre-order numbers, Apple evaluates the success of each launch and uses the insights to refine their approach for future product releases.

CASE STUDY 2: DOVE'S 'REAL BEAUTY' CAMPAIGN

Dove's 'Real Beauty' campaign focused on changing the conversation around beauty standards. The campaign's success was measured not just by media coverage but by the shift in public perception it generated. Dove tracked sentiment analysis, engagement metrics and brand affinity scores to evaluate the campaign's impact, which led to a significant increase in brand loyalty and sales.

CONCLUSION

Measuring PR success is both an art and a science. It requires a balance between quantitative data and qualitative insights. By focusing on the right KPIs, regularly evaluating your efforts and learning from each campaign, you can refine your PR strategy and continue to build a powerful, influential brand presence. Remember, PR is a long game, and success builds over time. So keep your eyes on the metrics, but don't lose sight of the bigger picture: building relationships, shaping public perception and, ultimately, creating a lasting impact.

11

WHY IS PR SO EXPENSIVE?!

When most people think of PR, they often imagine it's all about glitzy events, glossy magazine covers and charming publicists whispering into the ears of journalists over martinis. While that's part of the allure, the reality is that PR is much more than that: it is a complex, multifaceted discipline that requires a significant investment of time, resources and expertise. This is why PR can be expensive, yet it's why it's worth every penny.

THE REAL COST OF PR: MORE THAN JUST PRESS RELEASES

PR isn't just about writing a press release and crossing your fingers that it gets picked up by the media. If only it were that simple! The true cost of PR comes from the expertise, strategy and ongoing work required to build and maintain a strong public image.

1. Expertise and Experience

You are not just paying for someone to draft a few press releases; you are paying for years of experience, industry knowledge and the ability to navigate the media landscape effectively. PR professionals have spent years building relationships with journalists, editors, influencers and other key players in the industry. They understand the nuances of messaging, timing and audience engagement. This kind of expertise doesn't come cheap because it's the difference between getting a story picked up by a top-tier outlet or being ignored entirely.

2. Strategy Development

A successful PR campaign doesn't happen by accident; it requires careful planning, research and strategy development. PR professionals spend a significant amount of time understanding your brand, your goals and your target audience. They craft a tailored strategy that aligns with your business objectives and positions you effectively in the market. This strategic groundwork is crucial for long-term success, and it's one of the reasons PR requires a substantial investment.

3. Time and Effort

PR isn't a one-and-done activity; it is an ongoing process that requires constant effort. From media monitoring and relationship building to crafting pitches, organising events and managing social media, PR professionals are always working behind the scenes to keep your brand in the public eye. This level of dedication and the sheer amount of work involved is another reason why PR costs what it does.

4. Media Relations

Building and maintaining relationships with the media is no easy task. Journalists are bombarded with pitches every day, and it takes a skilled PR professional to cut through the noise and get your story noticed. These relationships don't happen overnight; they are built on trust, credibility and a history of delivering valuable content. A strong media relationship is an asset that can yield significant returns, but it requires time, effort and resources to cultivate.

5. Crisis Management

One of the often overlooked aspects of PR is crisis management. When things go wrong – and they will, eventually – it's your PR team that steps in to manage the fallout. Whether it's a bad review, a social media scandal or a full-blown crisis, your PR team will work to protect your reputation and navigate the situation with grace and professionalism. Crisis management requires a cool head, quick thinking and a deep understanding of public perception, all of which contribute to the overall cost of PR.

6. Integrated Campaigns

In today's digital world, PR is no longer confined to traditional media. A comprehensive PR strategy often includes a mix of traditional media, social media, content marketing, influencer partnerships and more. Coordinating these different elements into a cohesive campaign requires significant resources and expertise. An integrated approach amplifies your message and ensures consistency across all channels, but it adds to the cost of PR.

WHY YOU SHOULDN'T BE AFRAID OF THE INVESTMENT

Now that we've established why PR is expensive, let's talk about why it's worth the investment:

1. Long-Term Value

PR is an investment in your brand's long-term success. While the upfront costs may seem high, the benefits of a well-executed PR strategy far outweigh the expenses. PR helps build brand awareness, establish credibility and foster trust with your audience. These are invaluable assets that will serve your business for years to come.

2. Reputation Management

Your reputation is one of your most valuable assets, and PR is the key to managing and protecting it. In today's fast-paced, digitally connected world, a single negative story can spread like wildfire and do serious damage to your brand. A strong PR strategy not only helps you build a positive reputation but provides a safety net when things go wrong.

3. Amplified Reach

A good PR campaign can amplify your reach far beyond what you could achieve on your own. By leveraging media relationships, influencer partnerships and strategic content, PR can get your message in front of the right people at the right time. This kind of exposure is difficult to achieve through other means and can significantly boost your brand's visibility and credibility.

4. Credibility and Trust

One of the most powerful benefits of PR is third-party endorsement. When a respected journalist, influencer or media outlet talks about your brand, it carries far more weight than anything you could say about yourself. This kind of credibility is invaluable and it's one of the main reasons businesses invest in PR.

5. Return on Investment

While PR may not deliver immediate, measurable returns like a sales campaign, its impact is far-reaching and long-lasting. A successful PR campaign can lead to increased brand awareness, higher customer loyalty and, ultimately, more sales. It is important to view PR as a long-term investment that pays off over time rather than a quick fix.

6. Access to Opportunities

PR opens doors to opportunities that might otherwise be out of reach. Whether it's securing speaking engagements, landing media interviews or partnering with influential brands, PR can help you position yourself as an authority in your industry and open up new avenues for growth.

CONCLUSION: PR AS AN INVESTMENT IN YOUR FUTURE

Yes, outsourcing PR can be expensive, but the cost is reflective of the value it brings. It is an investment in your brand's reputation, credibility and long-term success. The benefits of a well-executed PR strategy far outweigh the costs, making it a worthwhile investment for any business serious about building a strong public presence.

I strongly believe that trying to 'save' money by not investing in PR is like saying you 'save' money on soap by not washing.

It is a false economy.

What you save in money, you lose in authority, credibility and brand equity, especially if you are one of many – in any industry. The higher the number of competitors in your market, the more PR will help elevate brand awareness, positioning and differentiation. Without PR, there are more opportunities to lose your market share to a bigger, shinier, more credible competitor.

PR may not seem like a priority when you have a good pipeline of leads... With that said, for many online businesses, all it would take is for a competitor to reverse hack your funnel and invest in higher ad spend than you to appear a viable alternative to your market. Add a publicity campaign to the mix and, in many instances, it becomes a no-brainer for your target market to choose to work with a more 'established' supplier than you. The more established your competition, the bigger the compound effect of a personal and business profile that transcends the bubble of social media.

The more sophisticated or further ahead in their business journey a buyer is, the more due diligence they will do on you and your business before investing, especially at high-ticket prices. This becomes even more prevalent during times of economic uncertainty. Buyers are inclined to invest in and with brands they know, recognise and trust, whether for personal or business use. Digital press coverage is one of the fastest ways to validate you as potential candidate. The more places your identity, expertise, credibility and authority can be validated both online and offline, the better.

Do not be afraid to invest in PR: it is one of the most powerful tools you have for shaping your brand's future. Also, don't think of PR as a spend that needs to provide instant ROI for your business.

Think of it more as an insurance policy, the effect of which appreciates and compounds over time.

12
MONETISING YOUR PR EFFORTS
TURNING VISIBILITY INTO REVENUE

One of the biggest concerns of almost every business owner I have ever encountered when it comes to PR is monetising their efforts, whether that be through increasing sales, securing investment or attracting sponsorship. As I said before, the purpose of PR is not to increase sales.

PR helps to establish trust and authority, which are crucial factors in a customer's decision-making process. When your brand is consistently visible in respected media outlets, endorsed by trusted third parties or associated with influential figures, it builds credibility and positions you as a leader in your industry. This in turn makes potential customers more likely to choose your products or services over competitors when they are ready to make a purchase.

Furthermore, PR can attract investment and sponsorship by enhancing your brand's image and reach. Investors and sponsors are more inclined to support businesses that have a strong public presence as it signals stability, market interest and potential for growth. PR helps create the narrative that appeals to these stakeholders, making your business an attractive prospect for financial backing.

In essence, while PR may not directly drive sales in the short term, it creates the conditions necessary for sustainable growth and profitability by enhancing your brand's visibility, credibility and appeal to both customers and financial backers.

In my nearly fifteen years as a publicist, I've seen countless businesses make the mistake of expecting PR to be a magic bullet for sales. They believe that one feature in a major publication or a single TV appearance will send their revenue through the roof in a matter of weeks. While PR is powerful, it's not a direct sales tool; it is a long game. The real value of PR lies in its ability to build credibility, enhance brand visibility and open doors to opportunities that, when leveraged correctly, can significantly increase your revenue.

Before I go into the best ways to effectively monetise your PR efforts, I need to reiterate something. It is not the role of PR to increase sales, revenue or your income. That is the job of your marketing and sales department (and, yes, I realise that might be you). The point is if you start your PR journey from the premise that you're going to make your investment back or become famous overnight, you'll end up bitterly disappointed.

One of the biggest misconceptions about PR is that the main ROI should be financial. If you've been paying attention to this point, you'll know that this is not the case.

If you're thinking of investing in PR on the basis that you have to make the money back almost immediately, not only is it likely that you aren't at the stage to invest, but that you don't understand that PR is a long-term, rather than short-term, revenue generating activity (RGA).

WHAT DOES THAT MEAN?

In order to foster sustainability in any area, be that growing a business, progressing your career or building a personal brand, we need to consider not just the short-term but the medium and long-term strategy.

Social media marketing, advertising and sales activity are short-term RGAs. For example, when you put out a post or Facebook ad with a call-to-action, an offer of a masterclass or a self-liquidating offer, or set up a sales funnel, the focus is on immediate conversion.

When you write a post to demonstrate your expertise, you should write blogs, build your mailing list or put yourself forward for podcast interviews to build credibility, authority and trust without asking for the sale. We understand that although these actions aren't likely to convert immediately, we are building towards a prospect potentially choosing us in the future.

Many small businesses learn the hard way or during a downturn that sustainable business requires not just short-term but medium and long-term revenue generation and growth strategies.

Unfortunately, long-term RGAs and growth strategies are the ones that a great number of smaller businesses tend to be *laissez-faire* about. In personal terms, PR and/or publicity is the life insurance policy or pension pot to ensure the longevity of your business.

Of course, you can be successful and grow a business without either. You may even cite HNWI as an example of those whose businesses can thrive without public attention.

This is true, although there are a few key things that people who are able to go under the radar tend to have that mere mortals don't:

A reputation/heritage that precedes them: Their name and what they do (their brand) is known by their target audience through family, personal or industry connections, which automatically confers authority, credibility and trust.

A powerful referral network: Word of mouth remains the most effective way to date to secure big business. All my six-figure contracts have come via word of mouth rather than marketing.

Proximity: One of the Ps of the AAA fame PR framework. In other words, borrowed or leveraged authority. Kim K famously capitalised on this by being papped as Paris Hilton's stylist and again during the leak of that tape with a more famous Ray J. It is also why people are still able to dine out on being invited to spend time with Branson on Necker Island.

Access: Sometimes money is the passport, other times it's your status (your personal brand) and the quality of your network.

There are some doors you'll never get you through if you aren't connected to the right people. Kim K was already in the right circles, thanks to her father, to even be in a position to capitalise on being Paris's stylist, all things that PR and publicity can help you develop over time. If you think PR and publicity are just about being in the public eye, you're completely missing the lesser cited but extremely valuable benefits of a well-thought-out strategy.

If you're in it for the long haul and are determined to make it to the big leagues but don't have a last name on the wing of an Ivy League university, you might want to rethink sleeping on PR.

The biggest ROI from PR is the relationships you build. The future opportunity value of relationships with new and current audiences, including the media and their publics. This is in addition to any real-time ROI, such as spikes in following, engagement, web traffic or even sales.

Does this mean you should only employ PR strategies when you need a boost? No. In the same way that marketing and content creation are seen as essential ongoing activities for sales, PR activity should be treated the same for relationship building.

If you were a baker, each member of your audience only needs a birthday cake for one day of the year, so it might take eleven months before they buy from you, but only if your bakery is top of mind (and trusted) for the other eleven months.

What is more, they have family and friends who have birthdays; they can buy cakes for them. They may even tell people about your bakery, share pictures of your cakes on social media for likes and shares and review them on Google.

Before you know it, your one customer has become eight. Your audience of one has become an audience of millions.

All because your bakery was top of mind.

'Top of mind' share is one of the most underrated benefits of consistent PR. This is why PR activity is most effective when undertaken as a long-term activity rather than a short-term solution.

1. MAXIMISING BRAND AWARENESS

PR is your stage. It is where you show the world who you are, what you stand for and why you're the best at what you do. But brand awareness alone doesn't pay the bills. To turn awareness into revenue:

- **Call to Action (CTA):** Every piece of PR, whether it's an interview, a guest article or a podcast appearance, should have a clear CTA. Guide your audience on what to do next, whether it's visiting your website, signing up for a newsletter or checking out a specific product.
- **Leverage Social Proof:** Use testimonials, media mentions and logos of the outlets that have featured you on your website and marketing materials. This not only boosts credibility but nudges potential customers towards making a purchase.

2. CREATING A FUNNEL FROM PR TO SALES

The best way to ensure your PR efforts lead to revenue is by creating a seamless funnel from awareness to conversion.

- **Lead Magnets:** Offer something valuable in exchange for your audience's contact information. It could be an eBook, a free consultation or a discount code. PR can drive traffic to this offer, which then feeds into your sales funnel.

- **Email Marketing:** Once you've captured leads through your PR efforts, nurture them through targeted email campaigns. Keep them engaged with updates, special offers and valuable content that builds a relationship and drives sales.
- **Retargeting Ads:** Use retargeting ads to reach people who have engaged with your PR content but haven't yet converted. This keeps your brand top of mind and increases the likelihood of conversion.

3. SECURING SPONSORSHIPS AND PARTNERSHIPS

PR doesn't just attract customers; it can attract potential sponsors and partners who want to associate with your brand.

- **Showcase Your Media Presence:** Sponsors and partners want to associate with brands that have visibility and credibility. Use your PR successes to demonstrate your reach and influence in the market. Highlight major media appearances, audience engagement and any significant endorsements.
- **Offer Collaborative Opportunities:** Reach out to potential sponsors with collaborative ideas. For example, if you've been featured in a prominent publication, suggest a joint venture where they sponsor your next event or webinar in exchange for brand mentions in your ongoing PR activities.
- **Leverage Events:** Use PR to promote events, whether they're physical or virtual, that can attract sponsors. Events give sponsors a platform to showcase their brand, while you benefit from the financial backing and the added credibility that comes with their association.

4. ATTRACTING INVESTORS

Investors are always looking for the next big thing, and a strong PR presence can be the key to grabbing their attention.

- **Build a Compelling Narrative:** PR allows you to craft and control the narrative around your business. Use this to your advantage by telling a compelling story about your growth, market potential and the impact you're making. Investors want to invest in more than just numbers; they want to invest in a vision.
- **Highlight Market Validation:** Use media coverage as proof of market interest and validation. If a reputable outlet has featured your business, it signals to investors that there's something noteworthy about your company. This can be a powerful tool in negotiations.
- **Showcase Leadership:** PR isn't just about your business; it is about you as a leader. Investors invest in people as much as they do in ideas. Use PR to highlight your expertise, vision and ability to steer the company towards success.

5. EXPANDING REVENUE STREAMS

PR can also be a powerful tool for expanding your revenue streams by introducing new products, services or even exploring new markets.

- **Product Launches:** Use PR to create buzz around new product launches. A well-timed press release, coupled with strategic media outreach, can create anticipation and drive initial sales.

- **Entering New Markets:** If you're expanding into new markets, PR can help you establish credibility quickly. Tailor your PR strategy to the new market by understanding local media landscapes and cultural nuances.
- **Upselling and Cross-Selling:** Leverage your PR efforts to highlight complementary products or services. For instance, if your PR campaign has brought attention to a particular product, use it as an opportunity to upsell or cross-sell related items.

6. LEVERAGING PR FOR SPEAKING ENGAGEMENTS AND THOUGHT LEADERSHIP

Becoming a thought leader in your industry can significantly boost your revenue. PR is your ticket to the stages where thought leaders are made.

- **Public Speaking:** Media coverage increases your visibility and credibility, making you a more attractive candidate for speaking engagements. These engagements can be lucrative revenue streams on their own, but they also position you as an authority, which can lead to further business opportunities.
- **Publishing Opportunities:** PR can open doors to publishing opportunities, whether it's a regular column in a reputable magazine or a book deal. Published content not only generates income but enhances your reputation, leading to more sales and partnerships.
- **Workshops and Webinars:** Use your PR platform to promote workshops, webinars and online courses. These not only generate direct revenue but create opportunities for upselling additional products or services.

7. MAXIMISING LONG-TERM RELATIONSHIPS

The real power of PR lies in building long-term relationships that continuously benefit your brand.

- **Media Relationships:** Cultivate strong relationships with journalists, influencers and media outlets. These relationships ensure that your brand remains in the public eye, leading to continuous opportunities for coverage, sponsorship and partnership.
- **Customer Loyalty:** PR isn't just about attracting new customers; it is about keeping the ones you have. Use PR to keep your audience engaged with your brand. Share your journey, milestones and updates to build a loyal community that supports your business over the long term.

CONCLUSION: PR AS AN INVESTMENT, NOT A COST

It is essential to shift your mindset from viewing PR as an expense to seeing it as an investment. When done correctly, PR lays the foundation for long-term success, opening doors to revenue streams that far exceed the initial investment. By strategically leveraging your PR efforts, you can create a powerful, revenue-generating machine that not only boosts your brand's visibility but drives sustained growth and profitability.

Remember, PR is about more than just getting your name in the paper or your face on TV; it is about crafting a narrative, building relationships and positioning yourself as a leader in your field. When you approach PR with a monetisation mindset, you'll not only see an increase in revenue but create a lasting impact that extends far beyond the initial buzz.

13
PRACTICAL TIPS AND BEST PRACTICES

So you've decided to dive into the world of PR and media engagement. Congratulations! This is a powerful step towards building your brand and expanding your influence. As with anything in life, preparation is key. In this chapter, we'll cover some practical advice for getting ready for PR, maintaining a positive public image and sustaining your fame and influence in the long run.

PRACTICAL ADVICE FOR PREPARING TO DO YOUR OWN PR AND MEDIA ENGAGEMENT

1. Know Your Story: Before you even think about pitching yourself to the media, you need to know your story inside and out. What makes you unique? What is the core message you want to communicate? This isn't just about your business or product; it is about the narrative that ties everything together. Spend some time refining your personal and brand story. Make sure it's compelling, authentic and resonant with your target audience.

2. Build Your Media Kit: A well-prepared media kit is your best friend when engaging with journalists and influencers. It should include:

- A brief bio or company overview
- High-quality headshots or product images
- Press releases or noteworthy news
- Links to previous media coverage
- Contact information

Make it easy for the media to understand who you are and what you're about and they'll be more likely to give you coverage.

3. Practice Your Pitch: Whether you're reaching out to a journalist, speaking on a podcast or doing a TV interview, you need to be able to pitch yourself confidently and succinctly. Practice delivering your pitch in different scenarios. Make sure it's clear, engaging and tailored to the person or outlet you're speaking to. Remember, the best pitches aren't just about what you want; they are about what you can offer to the audience.

4. Media Training: If you're new to media engagement, consider investing in some media training. This will help you get comfortable speaking to the press, answering tough questions and staying on message. Media training can also prepare you for the unexpected, like handling a tricky interviewer or dealing with technical issues during a live appearance.

5. Get Your Online Presence in Order: Your online presence is often the first thing people will check after hearing about you. Make sure your website is up to date, your social media profiles are polished and your content reflects your brand's message. Consistency is key: your online persona should match the image you're putting out through your PR efforts.

BEST PRACTICES FOR MAINTAINING A POSITIVE PUBLIC IMAGE

1. Be Authentic: People can spot a fake from a mile away. Authenticity is crucial for maintaining a positive public image. Do not try to be something you're not; embrace your true self, flaws and all. Audiences appreciate honesty, and being authentic will help you build a loyal following.

2. Stay Consistent: Consistency across your messaging, values and actions is vital. Whether it's through your social media posts, interviews or public appearances, make sure you're always reinforcing your core message. Consistency builds trust, and trust is the foundation of a positive public image.

3. Engage With Your Audience: Do not just talk at your audience; engage with them. Respond to comments on social media, acknowledge feedback and be approachable. People want to feel like they're part of your journey, so make an effort to connect with them on a personal level.

4. Handle Criticism Gracefully: Criticism is inevitable, especially as your visibility increases. The key is to handle it gracefully. Do not engage in public spats or defensive rants; take the high road. Address valid criticism with humility and use it as an opportunity to improve. For baseless attacks, sometimes the best response is no response at all.

5. Be Transparent: Transparency builds trust. If you make a mistake, own up to it. If you're changing direction, explain why. Being transparent with your audience helps maintain your credibility and shows that you're human.

6. Avoid Controversy, Unless it's Your Brand: Not every publicity is good publicity. Steer clear of unnecessary controversy unless your brand is built around challenging the status quo. Even then, be mindful of the battles you choose to fight. Make sure they align with your values and won't alienate your core audience.

LONG-TERM STRATEGIES FOR SUSTAINING FAME AND INFLUENCE

1. Evolve With Your Audience: The key to sustaining fame is evolution. As your audience grows and changes, you need to grow and change with them. Stay tuned into what your audience wants and needs and be willing to adapt your message and approach accordingly.

2. Diversify Your Channels: Do not rely on just one platform or type of media for your PR efforts. Diversify your channels: be active on social media, write guest posts, appear on podcasts and attend events. The more places your audience can find you, the stronger your influence will be.

3. Build Strategic Relationships: Long-term success in PR is often about who you know. Build and maintain relationships with key players in your industry: journalists, influencers, partners and other thought leaders. These relationships can open doors to new opportunities and keep you in the spotlight.

4. Invest in Personal Development: As you grow your brand, don't forget to grow yourself. Invest in personal development, whether it's through learning new skills, attending workshops or working with a coach. The more you grow, the more value you can offer to your audience.

5. Give Back: Use your influence for good. Engage in charitable work, support causes you care about and encourage your audience to do the same. Giving back not only strengthens your public image but enriches your life and builds a legacy.

6. Keep Innovating: The most influential figures are often those who aren't afraid to innovate. Do not get too comfortable: keep pushing the boundaries, trying new things and challenging yourself. Innovation keeps your brand fresh and ensures you remain relevant in a constantly changing world.

7. Monitor and Adjust: Finally, regularly monitor the effectiveness of your PR efforts. Track your key performance indicators (KPIs), evaluate what's working and what's not and be willing to adjust your strategy as needed. PR is not a set-it-and-forget-it game; it requires ongoing attention and adaptation.

Have you ever wondered what your followers really think about you and your brand?

Here is an exercise I ask my clients to do which will help uncover valuable insights through an accurate snapshot of how your audience perceives you:

Mini PR/Brand Gap Audit Activity:

Step 1: Spend five minutes thinking about how you wish your FB audience to perceive your brand.

Choose three values or attributes you believe you embody (and comes across on your posting) and one emotion you want people to feel when they land on your post or interact with you.

Step 2: Before you go asking anyone else what they think, take the time to review your last month of posting. Ask yourself if your content, photos and bio are 'giving' the four words you mentioned.

How? How not?

Look at what you share, the frequency, how accessible you are, the length of your posts and the photos and language you use.

Are you really showing up in the way you think you do?

Step 3: We are not stopping there.

The next stage is to set up an anonymous poll for your audience (check the last comment to see how to do this using Google Forms).

What do you notice about the responses?

CONCLUSION

PR is a powerful tool for building your brand, establishing your presence and expanding your influence, but like any tool, it's most effective when used with intention, preparation and care. By following these practical tips and best practices, you can ensure that your PR efforts not only yield immediate results but set you up for long-term success. Remember, PR is a journey, not a destination. Buckle up, stay true to yourself and enjoy the ride!

14
THE IMPACT OF AI ON PR TODAY AND THE FUTURE

Artificial intelligence (AI) has become a buzzword in just about every industry, and public relations (PR) is no exception. With rapid advancements in AI technology, the way PR is done is evolving at a breakneck pace. While AI offers many benefits, it's crucial to understand that it's not a magic bullet or a replacement for the nuanced expertise that comes from hiring a seasoned PR agency. In this chapter, we'll dive into the impact AI is having on PR today, what it could mean for the future and why human expertise is still irreplaceable.

THE BENEFITS OF AI IN PR

AI has brought a host of benefits to the PR world, making certain aspects of the job faster and more efficient. Here are a few ways AI is positively impacting PR:

1. Media Monitoring and Analysis: AI-powered tools can monitor media mentions, track brand sentiment and analyse the impact of PR campaigns in real time. These tools can process vast amounts of data quickly, giving PR professionals insights that would take hours, if not days, to compile manually. This means faster reaction times and more informed decision-making.

2. Content Creation: Some AI tools can generate press releases, blog posts and social media content with surprising accuracy. These tools use natural language processing to create content that aligns with your brand's voice and message, saving time on routine tasks. However, while AI can handle straightforward content, it lacks the creativity and nuance that human writers bring to more complex or sensitive topics.

3. Personalisation and Targeting: AI can help PR professionals better understand their audience by analysing data and predicting behaviour. This allows for more personalised and targeted campaigns, which can lead to higher engagement rates. For example, AI can help determine the best times to send out press releases or which media outlets are most likely to pick up a story.

4. Crisis Management: AI can be used to monitor online chatter for potential crises before they explode. By analysing patterns and keywords, AI can alert PR teams to brewing issues, allowing them to address problems proactively before they spiral out of control.

5. Paid Media and Ad Optimisation: AI is particularly strong when it comes to optimising paid media campaigns. It can analyse which ads are performing best, suggest adjustments and even automate bidding processes to get the most bang for your buck. This is where AI truly shines: helping you get more value from your advertising spend.

WHY AI ISN'T A REPLACEMENT FOR A PR AGENCY

As impressive as AI can be, it's important to remember that it's not a substitute for the human touch that a PR agency provides. Here is why:

1. AI Lacks Creativity and Emotional Intelligence: AI is excellent at processing data and performing repetitive tasks, but it struggles with creativity and emotional nuance. Crafting a compelling story, understanding the subtleties of human emotion and navigating complex relationships with media professionals are areas where AI falls short. PR is as much about building relationships as it is about communication, and that requires a human touch.

2. AI Can't Build Relationships: At its core, PR is about building and maintaining relationships with the media, influencers and the public. These relationships are built on trust, empathy and mutual understanding, qualities that AI simply doesn't possess. A good PR agency knows how to nurture these relationships over time, something AI can't replicate.

3. Software Often Focuses on Paid Media: Many AI tools are designed with paid media in mind, not earned media. While paid media is important, it's just one piece of the puzzle. Earned media – coverage that you don't pay for but earn through relationships and storytelling – is where true PR magic happens. AI can help with ad placement and optimisation, but it's not going to secure you that coveted feature in *The New York Times*.

4. The Risk of Over-Reliance: There is a temptation to rely too heavily on AI, especially because it can be cost-effective and efficient. However, over-reliance on AI can lead to cookie-cutter campaigns that lack the originality and depth needed to stand out in a crowded market. PR is about more than just numbers and data; it is about connecting with people on a deeper level.

5. It Is Not Always Cheaper: Good AI software isn't cheap, and the costs can add up quickly. Moreover, if you're using AI to manage paid media, you might find that the costs of running campaigns are higher than expected. While AI can save you time, it's important to remember that time saved doesn't always equate to money saved, especially if the results aren't what you'd hoped for.

THE IMPORTANCE OF RESEARCHING AI TOOLS

If you're considering using AI to enhance your PR efforts, it's essential to do your homework. Not all AI tools are created equal, and the market is flooded with options. Here is what to keep in mind:

1. Research Thoroughly: Take the time to compare different AI tools, read reviews and understand what each one offers. Look for case studies or testimonials from businesses similar to yours. Remember, if a tool seems too good to be true, it probably is.

2. Beware of Low-Cost Options: While it's tempting to go for the cheapest option, remember that you get what you pay for. Low-cost tools might not have the features you need or may deliver subpar results. Investing in quality tools is essential if you want to see real benefits.

3. Consider the Learning Curve: Some AI tools have a steep learning curve. Make sure you or someone on your team is prepared to invest in the time needed to learn how to use the software effectively. Sometimes, a tool that's harder to use initially can provide greater benefits in the long run.

WHEN DIY PR IS THE ONLY OPTION

If you're on a tight budget, DIY PR might be your only option. However, that doesn't mean you have to do it alone. Here is how to make the most of DIY PR:

1. Start With a Consultation: Even if you're planning to do PR yourself, consider booking a consultation with a PR specialist. A fresh pair of eyes on your strategy can make a world of difference. They can help you refine your approach, identify potential pitfalls and give you tips on how to maximise your efforts.

2. Focus on the Essentials: When doing DIY PR, focus on the essentials: building relationships, crafting compelling stories and targeting the right media outlets. AI tools can help you streamline the process, but the core of PR – connecting with people – remains the same.

3. Use AI as a Supplement, Not a Substitute: Use AI tools to supplement your efforts, not replace them. AI can handle the heavy lifting of media monitoring, content scheduling and ad optimisation, freeing you up to focus on the more creative and strategic aspects of PR.

CONCLUSION: THE FUTURE OF AI IN PR

AI is undoubtedly changing the PR landscape, offering new tools and techniques to enhance the way we communicate and connect with audiences. However, it's essential to approach AI with a balanced perspective. While it can offer significant benefits, it's not a replacement for the creativity, emotional intelligence and relationship-building that are the cornerstones of successful PR.

As AI continues to evolve, the best PR strategies will likely combine the strengths of AI with the irreplaceable human touch of a skilled PR professional. Whether you're working with an agency, using AI tools or doing it yourself, the key to successful PR is understanding that it's about more than just technology; it is about people. At the end of the day, people connect with people, not algorithms.

15

NON-TRADITIONAL PR

When most people think of PR, they imagine press releases, newspaper articles and appearances on television. While these traditional methods are still powerful tools for building a brand, the landscape of public relations has expanded significantly in recent years. With the rise of social media, podcasts, LinkedIn and other non-traditional platforms, there are now more ways than ever to reach your audience and build your brand. This chapter will explore the world of non-traditional PR, offering you strategies to leverage these newer channels to create lasting impact.

1. SOCIAL MEDIA: THE MODERN PR POWERHOUSE

Let's start with the obvious: social media. Platforms like Instagram, Twitter, TikTok and Facebook have revolutionised the way we connect with others, allowing for direct engagement with your audience like never before. Some people have built entire empires without ever stepping foot in a traditional media outlet. If your primary goal is to generate income, social media can be your goldmine. However, if your goal is to create a lasting impact, you'll need to think strategically about how you use these platforms.

The Reach a Million Strategy: If you're looking to make a significant impact, aim to reach a million people with your message. This doesn't necessarily mean you need a million followers; it is about the cumulative reach of your content. Whether it's through a viral post, strategic collaborations or consistent, valuable content, social media offers the potential to amplify your message far beyond your immediate network. This strategy involves careful planning, regular posting and a deep understanding of your audience's needs and interests.

Monetising Social Media: For those focused on the bottom line, social media can be a direct path to revenue. Whether through sponsored posts, affiliate marketing or selling your own products or services, these platforms offer numerous opportunities to monetise your influence. However, remember that while social media can be profitable, it's also a crowded space, so standing out requires creativity, authenticity and persistence.

2. DO WHAT YOU LOVE MOST

One of the most important aspects of PR is authenticity. In a world where people are bombarded with content, authenticity stands out. The best way to stay authentic? Do what you love. Whether it's writing, podcasting, speaking or networking, focus on the activities that light you up. Not only will you enjoy the process more, but your enthusiasm will be contagious, drawing people to you naturally.

Writing: If you love to write, consider starting a blog or contributing articles to industry publications. Writing allows you to showcase your expertise and establish yourself as a thought leader in your field. Consistently sharing valuable insights will attract readers who appreciate your perspective and, over time, you'll build a loyal audience.

Podcasts: Podcasts are a fantastic way to connect with your audience on a deeper level. They allow you to share your knowledge, interview experts and engage in meaningful conversations. Plus, podcasts can be repurposed into blog posts, social media content and more, maximising your reach.

Interviews and Commentaries: Seek out opportunities to be interviewed on podcasts, YouTube channels or by journalists. Offering expert commentary on current events or industry trends can position you as a go-to source for insights. The more you put yourself out there, the more your name will become associated with expertise in your field.

Speaking Engagements: If public speaking is your passion, aim to secure speaking engagements at industry conferences, webinars and workshops. Speaking allows you to connect with audiences in real time, and the impact of a well-delivered speech can be long-lasting. Plus, it's a great way to network with other industry professionals.

3. LINKEDIN: THE PROFESSIONAL PR PLAYGROUND

LinkedIn is often overlooked as a PR tool, but it's one of the most powerful platforms for professionals looking to build their personal brand. Unlike other social media platforms, LinkedIn is specifically designed for professional networking, making it an ideal place to showcase your expertise, connect with industry peers and engage with thought leaders.

Building Your LinkedIn Presence: Start by optimising your LinkedIn profile. Ensure that it's complete, professional and reflective of your personal brand. Regularly share content that showcases your expertise, whether it's articles, industry news or your own insights. Engage with others by commenting on their posts, joining relevant groups and connecting with people who share your interests.

Thought Leadership on LinkedIn: LinkedIn is a great platform to position yourself as a thought leader. Publish articles directly on LinkedIn, share your experiences and offer advice to others in your industry. Over time, this will help you build a reputation as an expert, attracting opportunities for collaboration, speaking engagements and even media coverage.

4. IN-PERSON NETWORKING: THE OLD-SCHOOL STRATEGY THAT STILL WORKS

In the age of digital everything, in-person networking might seem a bit old-fashioned, but it's far from obsolete. There is something powerful about face-to-face interactions that digital communication just can't replicate. Whether it's attending industry events, conferences or even informal meetups, in-person networking is a valuable tool for building relationships and growing your influence.

Choosing the Right Events: Not all networking events are created equal. Choose events that align with your goals and where you're likely to meet people who can help you achieve them. Whether it's a local business mixer, a national conference or an industry-specific workshop, be strategic about where you spend your time.

Making the Most of Networking Opportunities: When you attend events, don't just hand out business cards and hope for the best. Engage in meaningful conversations, ask questions and really listen to the people you meet. Follow up with the connections you make and look for ways to offer value to them, whether it's through introductions, sharing resources or providing advice.

Leveraging Your Network: Once you've built a network, don't let those connections go cold. Regularly reach out to your contacts, offer support and stay engaged with their work. The stronger your relationships, the more likely you are to receive referrals, opportunities and introductions to other influential people.

CONCLUSION

Non-traditional PR offers a world of possibilities for those willing to think outside the box. From social media and podcasting to LinkedIn and in-person networking, there are countless ways to build your brand and reach your audience without relying solely on traditional media outlets. The key is to stay authentic, focus on what you love and be strategic in your approach. Whether your goal is to generate income, make an impact or both, non-traditional PR can help you achieve it. So go ahead, embrace the new, the unconventional and the innovative in your PR strategy.

16
WHEN PR GOES WRONG

There is no tool as powerful as PR for building your brand, increasing your visibility and connecting with your audience, but like any tool, if not used properly, it can backfire. When PR goes wrong, the consequences can be swift and brutal, leaving your reputation and sometimes your business at risk. In this chapter, we'll explore some of the most common pitfalls in PR and how to navigate them, including being trolled, managing capacity and knowing when and how to apologise.

BEING TROLLED: NAVIGATING THE DARK SIDE OF PR

In today's hyper-connected world, trolls are an unfortunate reality. You can have the best intentions and craft a perfect message and still find yourself at the receiving end of online vitriol. One reason I don't advocate DIY PR is because of an experience I someone went through that caused such distress, they decided never to engage in publicity after that. The comments made by readers on this national article were vile. They attacked this person's appearance and that of their family. Another person was attacked for their appearance after celebrating financial success and another had a Facebook group of 70,000 people calling them names after a viral feature that funnily enough was responsible for taking their business to the next level. Trolls thrive on negativity, and are often more interested in tearing you down than engaging in any meaningful dialogue. Let's talk about how to handle them.

1. Don't Feed the Trolls: The number one rule when dealing with trolls is simple: don't engage. Trolls feed off attention and responding to them usually only escalates the situation. Instead of getting dragged into a public spat, focus on positive interactions with your audience. Take a leaf from Beyoncé's book, leave them to your community to deal with.

2. Use Humour to Deflect: Sometimes, a well-placed joke can defuse a troll's attack. If you feel comfortable, responding with humour can show that you're not taking the bait. Just be careful not to come across as dismissive or condescending – it's a fine line. One of my favourite deflections was when Chris Brown the US entertainer posted a photo with his children on IG. A follower saw this as a cue to state she didn't "want a man with multiple baby mammas". His response "Who said I was hiring ma'am? You say that like you had a chance" He didn't attack just jokingly put her in her place.

3. Block and Report: Most social media platforms allow you to block and report abusive users. If a troll is crossing the line into harassment, don't hesitate to use these tools. Protecting your mental health and maintaining a positive online environment should be your top priority.

4. Focus on Your Supporters: For every troll, there are likely dozens, if not hundreds, of people who appreciate your work and support you. Do not let the negativity of a few overshadow the positivity of many. Engage with your supporters, thank them for their encouragement and continue to provide value.

CAPACITY: THE DOUBLE-EDGED SWORD OF PR SUCCESS

PR is designed to increase your visibility, but what happens when that visibility leads to more business than you can handle? It is a good problem to have – until it's not. Overcapacity can lead to missed opportunities, poor customer experiences and even damage to your reputation.

1. Plan for Success: Before launching a PR campaign, make sure your business is ready for the potential influx of interest. Do you have the systems in place to handle a surge in inquiries or orders? Can your team manage an increase in workload without sacrificing quality? It is better to scale gradually than to be overwhelmed by sudden success.

2. Set Expectations: Be clear with your audience about what they can expect in terms of response times, availability and service delivery. If you're inundated with inquiries, communicate openly about any delays. People are generally understanding as long as they know what's going on.

3. Consider Temporary Help: If your PR efforts bring in more business than you can handle, consider hiring temporary help or outsourcing certain tasks. This can relieve pressure on your core team and ensure that you continue to deliver a high level of service.

4. Prioritise Your Core Customers: In times of overcapacity, prioritise your most loyal customers. Make sure they continue to receive the attention and service they've come to expect from you. Neglecting your existing customer base in favour of new business is a quick way to lose trust and loyalty.

APOLOGY: THE ART OF SAYING SORRY

No one's perfect, and sometimes, despite your best efforts, things go wrong. Maybe you misspoke in an interview, sent out a poorly worded press release or made a mistake that went viral for all the wrong reasons. When this happens, the best course of action is often a sincere and well-crafted apology.

1. Own up to it: The first step in any apology is to take responsibility. Do not try to shift blame or make excuses. Acknowledge what went wrong and how it affected others. This shows that you're accountable and willing to make things right.

2. Be Sincere: An apology should come from the heart. People can tell when you're being disingenuous, and a fake apology can do more harm than good. Be honest about your regret and express a genuine desire to learn from the mistake.

3. Address the Issue Directly: Be specific about what you're apologising for. Vague apologies can come across as evasive. If you made a mistake in a public statement, correct the record. If you caused harm, explain what steps you're taking to prevent it from happening again.

4. Make Amends: Actions speak louder than words. Whenever possible, follow up your apology with concrete actions to make things right. This could be anything from offering a refund or compensation to implementing new policies or practices to avoid similar issues in the future.

5. Move on: Once you've apologised and taken steps to address the issue, it's important to move on. Do not dwell on the mistake or let it define you. Learn from the experience but continue to focus on your goals and the positive impact you want to make.

CONCLUSION

When PR goes wrong, it can feel like the sky is falling, but with the right strategies and mindset, you can navigate these challenges and come out stronger on the other side. Whether you're dealing with trolls, managing capacity or issuing an apology, remember that every setback is an opportunity to learn, grow and refine your approach. After all, the road to success is rarely a straight line; it is how you handle the bumps along the way that truly defines your journey.

17

SECURING BRAND COLLABORATIONS

Securing brand collaborations can be a game-changer for your business. These partnerships can elevate your brand's visibility, credibility and reach. But how do you go about landing these coveted collaborations? This chapter will guide you through the steps to secure brand partnerships, whether you're just starting out or are an established business looking to expand your influence.

1. UNDERSTAND YOUR BRAND INSIDE AND OUT

Before you approach potential collaborators, you need to have a clear understanding of your own brand. Ask yourself:

- What are your brand's core values and mission?
- What makes your brand unique?
- Who is your target audience?
- What are your goals for this collaboration?

Knowing the answers to these questions will help you identify the right partners and craft a compelling pitch. Any collaboration should align with your brand's identity and long-term objectives.

2. IDENTIFY THE RIGHT PARTNERS

Not all collaborations are created equal. Just because a brand is well known doesn't mean it's the right fit for you. You need to find partners whose values, image and audience align with yours.

- **Complementary Brands:** Look for brands that complement yours rather than compete with it. For example, if you're a fitness brand, a collaboration with a healthy snack company could be a perfect match.
- **Audience Alignment:** Consider the brand's audience. Are they the same people you're trying to reach? If so, that's a good sign.
- **Reputation:** Research the brand's reputation. You want to partner with brands that are respected and trusted by their audience.

3. CRAFT A COMPELLING PITCH

Your pitch is your opportunity to sell your brand and the potential partnership. Here is what to include:

- **Value Proposition:** Explain why the collaboration would be beneficial for both parties. What is in it for them?
- **Your Brand's Story:** Share what makes your brand unique and why it stands out in the market.

- **Audience Insights:** Demonstrate that you understand their audience and how your brand would resonate with them.
- **Previous Successes:** If you've had successful collaborations in the past, highlight them to build credibility.
- **Specific Ask:** Be clear about what you're asking for, whether it's a co-branded product, a joint marketing campaign or something else.

4. BE PREPARED TO OFFER VALUE FIRST

In many cases, you may need to offer value before asking for anything in return. This could be in the form of:

- **Product Samples:** Sending a brand your product to try out before they agree to collaborate.
- **Exclusive Opportunities:** Offering them something unique, like an invitation to a VIP event or an exclusive preview of a new product.
- **Shared Content:** Creating content that highlights both brands and sharing it across your platforms.

The goal is to build a genuine relationship, not just a transactional one. The more value you can offer upfront, the more likely they are to want to work with you.

5. START SMALL IF NECESSARY

If you're just starting out, landing a major brand might feel out of reach. That is okay! Start with smaller, more accessible collaborations:

- **Local Brands:** Collaborating with local businesses can help you build credibility and establish your brand in a specific market before going after bigger names.
- **Niche Brands:** Partnering with niche brands can help you reach a targeted audience and create a strong brand association in your industry.
- **Micro-Influencers:** These influencers may have smaller followings, but they often have highly engaged audiences. They can be great partners for building your brand's reputation.

As you build your portfolio of successful collaborations, you'll be in a better position to approach bigger brands.

6. BUILD GENUINE RELATIONSHIPS

Sometimes, getting the attention of the right brands is as simple as being where they are:

- **Industry Events:** Attend events, conferences and trade shows where your target brands are likely to be. This gives you the chance to connect with them in person.
- **Online Communities:** Join online communities and forums where industry insiders hang out. This could be LinkedIn groups, industry-specific Facebook groups or other professional networks.

- **Social Media Engagement:** Engage with the brands you're targeting on social media. Comment on their posts, share their content and get on their radar.

Building these connections organically can lead to opportunities you might not have otherwise had access to.

7. HAVE A STRATEGY, NOT JUST TACTICS

Approach brand collaborations with a clear strategy in mind. This isn't just about landing one big partnership; it is about building long-term relationships that benefit your brand over time.

- **Set Clear Goals:** What do you hope to achieve through these collaborations? Is it brand awareness, increased sales or something else?
- **Develop a Plan:** How will you approach potential partners? What is your outreach strategy? How will you follow up and nurture these relationships?
- **Measure Success:** Determine how you'll measure the success of your collaborations. Are you looking at social media engagement, sales figures or media mentions?

By having a well-thought-out strategy, you'll be better positioned to secure meaningful partnerships that will help your brand grow and thrive.

CONCLUSION

Securing brand collaborations can be a transformative strategy for your business. It requires careful planning, persistence and a clear understanding of what you have to offer. Whether you're targeting local brands or major industry players, the key is to build genuine relationships, offer value and approach each partnership with a long-term mindset.

Remember, successful collaborations are about more than just a one-time partnership; they are about building lasting relationships that elevate your brand to new heights.

18
LANDING CELEBRITY CLIENTS

Landing a celebrity client can be a game-changer for your business. Celebrities bring a level of influence and visibility that can catapult your brand to new heights. Before you dream of red carpets and A-list endorsements, let's understand one thing: getting celebrity clients isn't about luck; it's about strategy, persistence and savvy networking. In this chapter, we'll walk through the steps you need to take to attract and secure celebrity clients.

1. KNOW THE IN AND BE PREPARED TO PAY

The first thing to understand about working with celebrities is that access often comes at a cost. Whether it's paying for introductions through trusted sources, investing in exclusive events or hiring a PR agency with exclusive access be prepared to put your money where your mouth is.

Trusted Sources: Celebrities typically operate within tight-knit circles. To break into these circles, you might need to pay for introductions or work with intermediaries who've already established relationships with the celebrities you're targeting. This could be PR agents, managers or other professionals in their orbit who can vouch for your credibility.

Be Prepared to Invest: Gaining access to the right events or networks may require a significant financial investment. For example, joining high-end networking groups, sponsoring exclusive events or even paying for a spot in elite charity galas can open doors to celebrity connections. Remember, this isn't just about the money; it is about showing that you're serious, credible and ready to play in their league.

2. GET PAST THE GATEKEEPER

Celebrities are busy people, who rarely manage their own schedules or communications. This is where the gatekeeper – often a personal assistant, manager or agent – comes into play. To get to the celebrity, you'll need to get past the gatekeeper.

Research and Personalise: Understand who the gatekeepers are and what they care about. When you reach out, make sure your pitch is tailored to the gatekeeper's interests or needs. Remember, they hear pitches all the time, so yours needs to stand out.

Respect Their Role: Gatekeepers hold the keys to the kingdom, and respecting their role is crucial. Be professional, patient and courteous in all interactions. Building a rapport with the gatekeeper can often be as important as building one with the celebrity.

Leverage Referrals: A referral from someone the gatekeeper trusts can fast-track your access. If you've built relationships with others in the celebrity's circle (more on this later), now's the time to leverage those connections.

3. BE PREPARED TO GIVE BEFORE ASKING (OR RECEIVE NOTHING IN RETURN)

Celebrities are inundated with requests, so before you ask for anything, be prepared to offer value first. This could mean offering your services for free (or at a discount) initially to demonstrate your expertise and build trust.

Offer Value First: Before you pitch your services, think about what you can offer that the celebrity might find valuable. Can you provide a unique service, introduce them to someone in your network or contribute to a cause they care about? The idea is to give without expecting anything in return – building goodwill often leads to bigger opportunities down the line.

Expect Nothing: Sometimes, despite your best efforts, your initial outreach might not lead to a partnership. That is okay. Building relationships, especially with high-profile clients, takes time. Stay persistent, keep providing value and be patient.

4. BUILD RELATIONSHIPS WITH PEOPLE IN THEIR CIRCLE

If you can't get to the celebrity directly, start by building relationships with the people in their circle. Celebrities trust their inner circle, and a strong recommendation from someone they know and respect can be invaluable.

Network Strategically: Identify the people who have influence over the celebrity's decisions. This could be their publicist, stylist, personal trainer or even close friends. Attend the same events, engage with them on social media and find ways to be helpful to them.

Create a Win-Win: When you build relationships with people in a celebrity's circle, think about how you can create win-win situations. For example, if you're a PR specialist, offer to help their stylist or trainer gain more exposure in exchange for an introduction to the celebrity.

Be Genuine: Celebrities and their teams are used to people trying to use them for personal gain. Approach these relationships with sincerity and a genuine interest in helping them achieve their goals. Authenticity goes a long way in building trust.

5. HANG OUT WHERE THEY DO

You are not going to meet a celebrity client sitting behind your desk. You need to be where they are, whether that's at exclusive events, luxury gyms, high-end restaurants or charity galas. Proximity is key.

Exclusive Events: Attend the same events as your target celebrity clients. These could be industry awards, charity fundraisers or even luxury product launches. The goal is to put yourself in their orbit and create opportunities for organic interactions.

Social Clubs and Networks: Join clubs, networks or organisations where celebrities and their teams are likely to hang out. Whether it's a private members' club, a high-end gym or an industry association, being part of the same community can naturally lead to introductions.

Be Social Media-Savvy: Celebrities often share their whereabouts on social media. While you shouldn't be a stalker, keeping an eye on their public appearances can help you strategically position yourself at the right place at the right time.

6. START FROM THE BOTTOM – OR THE TOP

When it comes to working with celebrities, there's more than one way to get your foot in the door. You can either start by working with up-and-coming stars or go straight for the top-tier celebs. Each approach has its own benefits.

Starting From the Bottom: Working with emerging celebrities can be a great way to build your reputation in the industry. As they rise, your association with them will increase your credibility and visibility. Plus, emerging celebs are often more open to working with new partners and may be easier to approach.

Going Straight for the Top: If you have the resources and connections, targeting A-list celebrities can be a high-risk, high-reward strategy. The visibility and credibility gained from working with top-tier celebs can be immense, but it requires a strong pitch, excellent timing and, usually, a significant investment.

Leverage Both Strategies: There is no rule that says you have to choose one path. You can start by building your reputation with emerging stars and, once you have some success stories, use that as leverage to approach bigger names.

7. HAVE A STRATEGY, NOT JUST TACTICS

Landing a celebrity client is not about scattershot tactics; it is about having a clear, well-thought-out strategy that aligns with your long-term business goals.

Define Your Objectives: What do you hope to achieve by working with a celebrity client? Is it brand visibility, credibility or access to new markets? Knowing your objectives will help you create a targeted strategy.

Craft a Compelling Pitch: Your pitch to a celebrity client needs to go beyond the basics. It should be a well-researched, compelling narrative that clearly explains why working with you will benefit them. Show how you understand their brand, their audience and how your services can enhance their image or reach.

Be Patient and Persistent: Securing a celebrity client doesn't happen overnight; it requires patience, persistence and a willingness to keep refining your approach. Keep showing up, keep offering value and, eventually, the right opportunity will present itself.

Measure Success: Once you've landed a celebrity client, don't rest on your laurels. Continuously measure the success of your campaigns, adapt your strategies and ensure that the relationship remains mutually beneficial.

CONCLUSION

Getting celebrity clients is no small feat, but with the right strategy, persistence and a little bit of luck, it's entirely achievable. Remember, celebrities are people too: they have goals, challenges and needs just like any other client. By understanding their world, offering genuine value and building trust, you can turn your dream of working with celebrity clients into a reality. Who knows? The next red-carpet event you attend might just be as a trusted advisor to the stars.

19

BLOWING UP: HOW TO DEAL WITH GOING VIRAL

Going viral: two words that will either send shivers down your spine or fill you with excitement. In today's socially connected world, the internet can turn you into an overnight sensation. While the prospect of going viral might seem like the golden ticket to fame and success, it's important to remember that it comes with its own set of challenges. This chapter is all about preparing you for that moment when the internet decides to make you famous, whether you're ready for it or not.

1. THE VIRAL ROLLER COASTER

First things first, going viral is like strapping yourself into a roller coaster that you never actually agreed to ride. One minute, you're casually posting content online, and the next, you're being flooded with notifications, messages and comments. It can feel exhilarating, but also overwhelming.

Embrace the Ride, but Hold on Tight: When you go viral, it's easy to get caught up in the whirlwind of attention. Enjoy the moment, but remember to stay grounded. The buzz will die down eventually, so it's important to keep your focus on your long-term goals rather than getting swept away by temporary fame.

Do Not Let the Pressure Get to You: With virality comes pressure: pressure to maintain the momentum, to keep creating content that people love and to live up to the newfound expectations. It is crucial to remember that not every piece of content will go viral, and that's okay. Keep doing what you do best and don't let the pressure push you into a creative burnout.

2. MANAGING THE FLOOD OF ATTENTION

When your content blows up, you'll likely find yourself inundated with new followers, comments and inquiries. While this can be great for building your audience, it can also be overwhelming if you're not prepared.

Set Boundaries Early on: As your online presence grows, so will the demands on your time and energy. It is important to set boundaries from the get-go. Decide how much time you're willing to spend responding to comments and messages and stick to it. You don't have to engage with every single person who reaches out. Prioritise the interactions that matter most.

Delegate if Possible: If the influx of attention becomes too much to handle, consider delegating some of the work. Whether it's hiring a social media manager to help you manage your accounts or bringing on a PR professional to handle media inquiries, having support can help you navigate the chaos without burning out.

Engage Authentically: While you can't respond to everyone, it's important to engage authentically with your audience. Show appreciation for their support, answer questions when you can and be genuine in your interactions. Authenticity goes a long way in building a loyal following.

3. HANDLING THE CRITICS

Let's be real, going viral isn't all sunshine and roses. With the flood of attention, you're also likely to encounter critics, trolls and people who just aren't fans of your work. It can be tough to deal with negativity, especially when it's coming at you in droves.

Do Not Take it Personally: The internet can be a harsh place and not everyone will like what you do. It is important to remember that criticism often says more about the critic than it does about you. Do not take negative comments to heart; focus on the positive feedback and constructive criticism instead.

Choose Your Battles Wisely: Not every comment deserves a response. While it can be tempting to clap back at trolls, it's often best to just ignore them. Engaging with negativity can escalate the situation and draw even more unwanted attention. Instead, save your energy for meaningful interactions.

Lean on Your Support System: Dealing with criticism can be emotionally draining, so it's important to lean on your support system. Whether it's friends, family or a trusted colleague, having people who can offer encouragement and perspective will help you navigate the rough patches.

4. CAPITALISING ON THE MOMENTUM

Going viral is a rare opportunity, and if you play your cards right, it can open doors for you that you never imagined. The key is to capitalise on the momentum without losing sight of your long-term goals.

Ride the Wave: Once you've gone viral, don't just sit back and let the moment pass you by; use it as a springboard for your next move. Whether it's launching a new product, promoting a service or simply increasing your visibility, take advantage of the attention while you have it.

Stay True to Your Brand: It can be tempting to shift gears and start creating content that's solely focused on maintaining virality. However, it's important to stay true to your brand and your message. Remember why you started in the first place and keep that at the forefront of everything you do.

Turn One-Time Viewers Into Long-Term Followers: The ultimate goal of going viral is to convert one-time viewers into loyal followers. Encourage your new audience to follow you on social media, subscribe to your newsletter or check out your website. Offer them something of value, whether it's exclusive content, a discount or just more of the content they love.

5. PLANNING FOR THE FUTURE

Once the viral moment has passed, it's time to focus on the future. Going viral can be a game-changer, but it's what you do afterward that really counts.

Keep the Momentum Going: While the initial buzz may die down, that doesn't mean your work is done. Continue creating and sharing content that resonates with your audience. Consistency is key to maintaining your newfound popularity and turning it into long-term success.

Evaluate What Worked: Take some time to evaluate what led to your viral success. Was it the content itself? The timing? The platform? Understanding what worked will help you replicate that success in the future and refine your PR strategy.

Do Not Rely on Virality Alone: Going viral is great, but it's not a sustainable strategy on its own. Make sure you're building a solid foundation for your brand with consistent PR efforts, whether that's through social media, traditional media or other channels.

CONCLUSION

Going viral can be a great experience, but it's not without its challenges. By remaining grounded, managing the influx of attention, handling criticism with grace and capitalising on the momentum, you can turn a viral moment into lasting success. Remember, while virality is a powerful tool, it's just one piece of the PR puzzle. Keep your focus on your long-term goals and use your viral success as a stepping stone to even greater achievements.

20

THE FUTURE OF PR

As we step into a new era, the landscape of public relations (PR) is undergoing a profound transformation. This isn't just a shift in strategies or tools; it's a seismic change in how we approach communication, influence and connection on a global scale. The world is moving from a unipolar reality, where a single narrative often dominated, to a multipolar world, where multiple voices, perspectives and centres of power coexist and compete. This chapter explores how these changes are reshaping PR and what that's likely to mean for the future of the industry.

CHANGING DYNAMICS: FROM UNIPOLAR TO MULTIPOLAR REALITY

For the longest time, PR was like a well-rehearsed orchestra, with a few big players – the media conglomerates – conducting the narrative. They decided what stories were told, how they were told and who got to hear them. This unipolar approach made it easy to control the narrative, but it also meant that many voices went unheard.

However, as the world transitions to a multipolar reality, this centralised model is breaking down. The rise of social media, citizen journalism and decentralised platforms means that everyone now has a voice and the ability to influence public discourse. It is like the orchestra has been replaced by a global jam session: everyone's contributing, and while it can get a bit chaotic, it's also more inclusive and democratic.

But here's the thing: each individual news centre is just that: a centre. This means that truth will always be seen through the lens of the person 'reporting'. Seeing what is taking place in real time through the eyes of another doesn't give the whole picture. It doesn't zoom out, nor does it provide history or context; it just gives their snapshot. Imagine a group of people standing in a circle, each taking a photo at one-degree intervals. We would end up with three-hundred and sixty different vantage points, each showing a slightly different perspective of the same scene.

In this new world, there is a need to move beyond the idea of outsourcing verification to a single source; instead, we must embrace the concept of decentralised truth contributing to a community truth. With the advancement of AI, it's becoming clear that one person's truth is not enough. There will always be a need for collective truth to 'verify' what applies to the collective as one person's truth doesn't stand true for all. Otherwise, we replace one centralised figure (traditional media) with another (a social media reporter). Every system has its benefits and downfalls.

DECENTRALISED PR: A NEW APPROACH

As PR evolves, we're moving towards a decentralised model, much like the trends we're seeing in AI and finance - think Bitcoin and Blockchain. This decentralised approach means that instead of relying on a top-down or bottom-up structure, we're looking at a network where each individual or entity – plays a role in shaping the narrative. This shift requires us all to think differently about how they craft and disseminate messages.

In a decentralised world, connection becomes more important than control. The old methods of managing narratives from a central point of power are no longer effective. Today's audiences are more educated, more sceptical and demand authenticity and transparency. They can see through the spin and they're quick to call out anything that feels inauthentic.

CONNECTION OVER CONTROL

One of the most significant shifts in modern PR is the move from controlling the narrative to creating genuine connections. Audiences today are more educated and sceptical than ever before. They can see through the old tricks of spin and manipulation. What they crave is authenticity and transparency.

For media professionals, this means shifting from a mindset of control to one of connection. It's about being real, honest and relatable. It is about building trust through consistent, genuine interactions rather than flashy, one-off campaigns. In this new world, the most successful PR efforts will be those that resonate on a human level, fostering deep connections rather than superficial engagements.

SPIRITUAL AND COSMIC INFLUENCES: THE ENERGETIC DIMENSION OF PR

Here is where things get a little woo. Literally. The changes we're seeing in PR are not just happening on a surface level; they are part of a broader shift in consciousness and energy that's affecting everything, from how we think to how we communicate.

The cosmos, with its vast, unseen forces like dark energy and dark matter, serves as a metaphor for the invisible influences in PR. Just as these cosmic forces shape the universe, unseen energies shape public perception and communication. Understanding these forces means recognising that PR isn't just about the visible; it is about the subtle, the energetic and the spiritual.

This spiritual insight into PR encourages professionals to tap into deeper levels of awareness. It is about understanding the energetic undercurrents that influence public opinion and learning to work with them rather than against them.

EVOLVING CONSCIOUSNESS: BREAKING DOWN THE OLD PARADIGM

The traditional left-brain, patriarchal approach to PR – focused on logic, control and dominance – is breaking down. In its place, a new consciousness is emerging. This new paradigm is more holistic, more connected and more inclusive. It is about balancing the left-brain strategies with right-brain creativity, intuition and empathy.

For PR, this means evolving from the old ways of doing things. It is about embracing a more integrated approach that considers not just the message but the messenger, the audience and the broader context in which communication occurs.

THE ROLE OF PR: SHAPING THE FUTURE, NOT JUST MANAGING THE PRESENT

In this new era, PR is no longer just about managing attention or controlling a narrative; it is about shaping trajectories and creating futures. Effective PR will involve tapping into and seeding positive consciousness, planting ideas and messages that not only resonate in the present but influence the future direction of public thought.

This forward-thinking approach requires a deep understanding of where the world is heading and the ability to align PR strategies with these emerging trends. It is about being proactive, not reactive, and using PR as a tool to help clients not just navigate the present but shape the future.

CHALLENGES AND OPPORTUNITIES: NAVIGATING THE NEW LANDSCAPE

As with any major shift, the transition to this new paradigm comes with both challenges and opportunities. One of the biggest challenges will be discerning truth from falsehood in a world where information is increasingly decentralised and fragmented. The battle between centralised and decentralised models of communication will play out in the media world, and those who can navigate this tension will be the most successful.

At the same time, there are tremendous opportunities for those willing to embrace these changes. The ability to build genuine connections, foster trust and shape the future of communication is within reach for those who are open to this new way of thinking.

INTERNAL AUTHORITY: BUILDING FROM THE INSIDE OUT

One of the key insights of this new PR approach is the importance of internal authority. For PR to be effective, it must reflect a deep internal alignment with the client's true self and purpose. This involves understanding and transforming personal narratives and wounds and helping clients project their authentic selves into the world.

I predict PR professionals will need to guide clients through this process of internal transformation, helping them build the internal authority that will then be reflected externally. This is not just about crafting a message; it is about helping clients embody the message.

VISUAL SILENCE: THE POWER OF DISCONNECTING

In a world where we're constantly bombarded with images, messages and reflections of ourselves, creating moments of visual silence is crucial. This is about taking a step back, disconnecting from the noise and reconnecting with internal truths. By creating space for visual silence, we regain clarity on what truly matters, allowing us to craft messages that are not just effective but authentic and meaningful. This practice is essential for all of us to ensure we operate and create from a place of integrity and authenticity.

HOLISTIC APPROACH: INTEGRATING SPIRITUAL INSIGHTS INTO PR

The future of PR will involve a more holistic approach, integrating spiritual insights and practices into the process. This means recognising the interconnectedness of all elements, from the message, to the medium, to the audience. It is about understanding that everything is connected and that true success comes from working with these connections rather than against them.

CHAOS AND CREATIVITY: EMBRACING THE UNKNOWN

Finally, the future of PR will require a willingness to embrace chaos and the creative potential it brings. In a rapidly changing world, the ability to navigate uncertainty and turn it into an opportunity will be a key skill. PR professionals will need to guide clients through transitional phases, helping them harness their inner chaos and turn it into creative power.

MASTERING THE TENSION: GUIDING CLIENTS THROUGH BREAKTHROUGHS

As clients navigate these shifts, they will inevitably face tension points: moments where their desires clash with internal blockages or external realities. PR professionals must help clients process through these moments, guiding them towards true breakthroughs.

This process of mastering the tension is where real transformation happens. It is about helping clients move beyond their fears and limitations and step into their true potential as leaders, influencers and change-makers.

THE RISE OF PURPOSE-DRIVEN PR

Consumers are increasingly drawn to brands that stand for something. Social responsibility and brand values are no longer just nice-to-have—they're essential. In the future, PR will need to evolve to prioritise purpose-driven messaging. This will mean aligning brands with causes that resonate with their audience and advocating for social, environmental, or ethical issues. Brands that can authentically demonstrate their commitment to something beyond profit will have the upper hand.

AI AND MACHINE LEARNING IN PR STRATEGY

AI's future role in PR will continue to grow beyond just data processing. Machine learning will become central to predicting media trends, audience behaviour, and even crafting tailored content that speaks directly to individual user preferences. AI won't replace creativity, but it will automate more of the administrative and data-driven tasks, allowing PR professionals to focus on strategic, human-driven activities.

IMMERSIVE EXPERIENCES AND VIRTUAL REALITY

With the rise of virtual reality (VR) and augmented reality (AR), PR will need to embrace immersive storytelling. Brands will likely use VR and gamification to create experiences that allow consumers to interact with their products, missions, or stories in a more personal and engaging way.

BLOCKCHAIN AND PR TRANSPARENCY

As blockchain technology matures, it could have an impact on PR through enhanced transparency. Blockchain can provide verifiable data trails, ensuring that news and information shared by brands or media professionals can be authenticated and trusted. This technology could play a role in reducing the spread of misinformation and build more trust between brands and their audiences.

THE HUMAN TOUCH IN AN AUTOMATED WORLD

While automation and AI will continue to expand, the need for authentic human interaction will only grow. PR will remain rooted in relationships—building trust and rapport with journalists, influencers and the public. The future of PR will require balancing high-tech solutions with high-touch human elements, ensuring that personal connections and authentic storytelling remain at the forefront.

HYPER-PERSONALISATION OF CONTENT

The future of PR will increasingly focus on hyper-personalisation, where messages are not just tailored to specific demographics but to individuals. PR professionals will use data and AI to craft highly personalised content that speaks to the specific interests, behaviours, and emotions of individual audience members. This shift will result in higher engagement and stronger relationships between brands and consumers.

INFLUENCER EVOLUTION

While influencers are already key players in PR strategies, the influencer landscape will continue to evolve. Micro-influencers and niche influencers will grow in importance as brands seek more authentic and targeted connections with their audiences. Furthermore, AI-powered virtual influencers (completely digital personas) are on the rise and will continue to play a role in the future of brand representation.

ETHICAL PR AND CRISIS MANAGEMENT

As brands face greater scrutiny from the public, ethical PR will become even more critical. In an era of cancel culture, where social justice movements hold brands accountable, PR professionals will need to help companies navigate these ethical waters carefully. Building ethical frameworks and crisis management strategies will be at the forefront of every PR plan in the future.

CROSS-PLATFORM INTEGRATION

PR campaigns of the future will need to be seamlessly integrated across multiple platforms. A campaign may launch on traditional media, but it will also need to engage audiences through social media, podcasts, influencer partnerships, and virtual events. The ability to create unified messages across varied platforms will be a hallmark of effective PR strategies in the future.

THE POWER OF COMMUNITIES

I predict that PR will increasingly move toward fostering and growing communities rather than just large audiences. Brands will need to focus on creating loyal and engaged groups of people who not only consume their content but advocate on their behalf. These communities will serve as powerful voices for the brand and will help in creating more sustainable, long-term relationships.

PERSONAL TRANSFORMATION: THE HEART OF FUTURE PR

At its core, I believe the future of PR will play a key role in personal transformation, helping clients not just communicate their message, but become the message. My aim will be to guide clients through a journey of self-discovery and growth, helping them emerge as their most authentic, powerful selves.

For all PR and comms professionals, this shift will mean embracing their role not just as a strategist but as guides, mentors and a catalyst for change. The success of future PR will be linked to their ability to navigate and support these transformations, helping clients achieve not just their PR goals but their highest potential. I for one can't wait for this to be standard protocol. My desire has always been to keep humanity at the heart of PR.

YOUR JOURNEY TOWARDS CELEBRITY, IMPACTFUL FAME AND LEGACY

As we reach the end of this journey together, it's time to take a moment to reflect upon everything we've covered. This book has been a guide, a mentor and perhaps even a bit of a cheerleader for you as you've navigated the complex world of public relations and the power of fame. My goal has been to help you understand not just the mechanics of PR but the deeper, more transformative potential that lies in strategically managing your public image.

We have explored the evolution of PR, the importance of third-party endorsements and the many ways in which PR can serve as a powerful tool for personal and professional growth. From understanding the media landscape to leveraging your unique voice in a crowded marketplace, we've delved into the heart of what it means to not only be seen but remembered for the impact you make.

The world of PR is vast and constantly changing, but at its core, it remains about one thing: connection. It is about connecting with your audience, with the media and, ultimately, with your own authentic self. The most successful PR strategies are those that are rooted in truth, transparency and a genuine desire to make a difference.

As you move forward, remember that PR isn't just about getting your name in the headlines; it is about crafting a legacy that will stand the test of time. It is about using your influence to not just benefit yourself but uplift others, drive change and leave a lasting mark on the world.

The journey of fame and visibility is not always easy. It requires courage, self-awareness and a willingness to be vulnerable. But it's in these challenges that you'll find your greatest opportunities for growth. Embrace them. Lean into the discomfort and trust that you are being shaped into the person you need to be to fulfil your purpose.

Now, I want to leave you with a final thought, a passage that speaks to the heart of everything we've discussed:

> *In life, you'll encounter spaces you feel aren't for you and opportunities you don't feel qualified for.*
> *Everything that's gone before will reinforce the belief that 'that's just the way things are'.*
> *It is in those moments, where you want to walk away, where the easier path beckons to play your role in maintaining the status quo...*
> *It is in those exact moments, fate extends an invitation, an opportunity to change the course of your life and, in turn, the lives of others by simply accepting the call to forge a new way.*
> *To go first.*
> *It is in those seemingly inconsequential moments, you'll look back at and realise instead of running away from destiny, you ran towards it.*
> *You chose to be part of a legacy greater than yourself.*
> *A catalyst for change.*
> *In doing so, life will forever be infinitely richer because of it.*

This passage encapsulates the essence of what I hope you take away from this book. You have the power to be a catalyst for change, to shape not just your own destiny but the destinies of those around you. By stepping into your full potential and embracing the visibility that comes with it, you can create a legacy that transcends time.

So, as you close this book and continue on your journey, I encourage you to carry this message with you. Let it be a reminder that the path to impactful fame is not just about being seen; it is about being seen for who you truly are and what you stand for. It is about making a difference one authentic step at a time.

Thank you for allowing me to be a part of your journey. Here is to the incredible legacy you're about to create.

APPENDICES

The appendices serve as a valuable resource to complement the main content of this book. Here, you'll find additional insights, practical tools and further reading that can help you implement the strategies discussed.

APPENDIX A:
GLOSSARY OF PR TERMS

Here's a glossary of key terms that have been used throughout the book:

GLOSSARY

1. Brand:

The identity of a business, individual or product that distinguishes it from others. This includes the name, logo, messaging and overall reputation that resonates with the target audience.

2. Brand Equity:

The value derived from consumer perception of the brand name rather than the product or service itself. Strong brand equity leads to customer loyalty and higher sales.

3. Brand Awareness:

The extent to which consumers are familiar with a brand and can recall or recognise it. High brand awareness is crucial for a brand's success.

4. Crisis Management:

The process of handling and mitigating the impact of an unexpected and potentially damaging event that affects a company's or individual's reputation.

5. Earned Media:

Publicity gained through organic efforts, such as media coverage, word of mouth or social media mentions, rather than paid advertising.

6. Influencer Marketing:

A strategy that involves partnering with individuals who have a large and engaged following on social media to promote a brand, product or service.

7. Integrated PR:

A holistic approach to PR that combines traditional media, digital media, social media, content marketing and other communication channels to create a cohesive and powerful brand message.

8. Key Performance Indicators (KPIs):

Metrics used to evaluate the effectiveness of PR campaigns. Common KPIs include media mentions, social media engagement, website traffic and brand sentiment.

9. Media Kit:

A collection of promotional materials provided to journalists and media outlets. It typically includes a press release, company background, key facts and high-quality images.

10. Media Relations:

The practice of building and maintaining relationships with journalists, editors and other members of the media to secure coverage and positive exposure for a brand or individual. Not the be mistaken for PR as a whole.

11. Narrative:

The overarching story or message that a brand or individual conveys to its audience. A strong narrative helps shape public perception and drives engagement.

12. Paid Media:

Any form of media coverage or exposure that is paid for, including advertising, sponsored content and paid influencer partnerships.

13. PESO Model:

A framework developed by Gini Dietrich that categories media into four types: paid, earned, shared and owned. This model helps create an integrated and balanced PR strategy.

14. Pitch:

A brief proposal or suggestion made to journalists or media outlets, often used to secure interviews, features or other types of media coverage.

15. PR (Public Relations):

The strategic communication process that builds mutually beneficial relationships between organisations or individuals and their publics. PR is focused on managing reputation and influencing opinion.

16. Press Release:

An official statement issued to the media to announce something newsworthy, such as a product launch, event or significant achievement.

17. Reputation Management:

The practice of influencing and controlling a brand's or individual's reputation, particularly online, by managing reviews, social media and public perception.

18. SEO (Search Engine Optimisation):

The process of improving the visibility of a website or web page in search engine results through various strategies, including the use of relevant keywords and high-quality content.

19. SERPs (Search Engine Results Pages):

SERPs refer to the pages displayed by search engines like Google in response to a user's search query. They consist of both organic results (unpaid) and paid results (advertisements). Ranking high on SERPs is a crucial goal for businesses and brands, as it increases visibility and credibility, which is why optimising for SEO (Search Engine Optimisation) is so important in PR and digital marketing strategies. The goal is to have your brand appear as close to the top of the first page as possible when relevant search terms are used and to dominate as much of the first page as possible.

20. Social Proof:

The concept that people are influenced by the actions and endorsements of others. In PR, social proof is often leveraged through testimonials, reviews and third-party endorsements.

21. Stakeholders:

Individuals or groups that have an interest in or are affected by the actions of a business or individual. Stakeholders can include customers, employees, investors and the media.

22. Thought Leadership:

The process of establishing a brand or individual as an expert or authority in a specific field through content creation, public speaking and media engagement.

23. Third-Party Endorsement:

When an independent source, such as a journalist, influencer or satisfied customer, speaks positively about a brand, product or service, adding credibility and trust.

24. Viral Marketing:

A marketing strategy that encourages individuals to share a message or campaign quickly and widely, typically through social media, to achieve rapid and widespread exposure.

25. Visual Silence:

The practice of disconnecting from visual stimuli (e.g., screens, social media) to focus on internal truths and gain clarity on messaging and strategy.

26. Word of Mouth:

The process of sharing information or opinions about a product or service through conversation, often leading to organic and trusted referrals.

APPENDIX B: SAMPLE PR CAMPAIGN TIMELINE

A successful PR campaign is carefully planned and executed over time. Below is a sample timeline for a 3 month campaign to guide you through the process, from initial research to final evaluation.

Week 1 to 2: Initial Research and Planning

Goal Setting: Define the objectives of the PR campaign (e.g., brand awareness, product launch, reputation management).

Audience Identification: Identify your target audience and understand their needs, preferences and media consumption habits.

Media Research: Compile a list of relevant media outlets, journalists, bloggers and influencers who align with your goals and target audience.

Message Development: Craft your core message and key talking points that will resonate with your target audience.

Strategy Development: Determine the tactics you'll use (e.g., press releases, media outreach, events, influencer partnerships).

Week 3 to 4: Content Creation and Media Kit Preparation

Press Release Drafting: Write a compelling press release that aligns with your campaign's goals.

Media Kit Assembly: Prepare your media kit, including the press release, fact sheet, company backgrounder and high-quality images.

Pitch Development: Create tailored pitches for different media outlets based on their focus and audience.

Week 5 to 6: Media Outreach and Campaign Launch

Pitch Distribution: Start sending out pitches and press releases to your targeted media list.

Follow-Up: Monitor responses and follow up with journalists and influencers who showed interest.

Event Planning: If applicable, finalise details for any events, webinars or product launches associated with the campaign.

Week 7 to 8: Campaign Execution

Event Execution: Host your event or launch, ensuring that all logistics are in place and media are accommodated.

Social Media Engagement: Amplify your message on social media through posts, stories and influencer collaborations.

Ongoing Media Relations: Continue engaging with the media, providing additional information, interviews or quotes as needed.

Week 9 to 10: Monitoring and Adjustments

Media Monitoring: Use media monitoring tools to track coverage, mentions and sentiment.

Engagement Analysis: Assess how your audience is responding to the campaign on social media and other platforms.

Mid-Campaign Adjustments: Make any necessary adjustments to your strategy based on media feedback and engagement metrics.

Week 11 to 12: Evaluation and Reporting

Campaign Evaluation: Measure the success of your campaign against the initial goals. Consider media coverage, audience reach, engagement and any leads or sales generated.

Reporting: Compile a comprehensive report summarising the outcomes, key takeaways and areas for improvement.

Thank Yous and Relationship Building: Send thank you notes to journalists, influencers and partners who supported your campaign. Nurture these relationships for future PR efforts.

APPENDIX C:
MEDIA KIT CHECKLIST

A media kit is an essential tool in any PR campaign, providing journalists and influencers with the information they need to cover your brand. Here's a checklist to help you create an effective media kit:

1. Press Release

2. Company Fact Sheet:

A concise document that provides key information about your company, product or event.

3. Company Backgrounder:

A more detailed document that outlines your company's history, achievements and vision.

4. High-Quality Images:

A selection of high-resolution images that journalists can use in their coverage, such as: Product images, executive headshots, Event photos, logos in various formats

5. Executive Bios:

Short bios of key executives, including their background, role in the company and any relevant quotes.

6. Case Studies or Success Stories:

Brief overviews of how your product or service has positively impacted customers or clients.

7. Testimonials or Endorsements:

Quotes from satisfied customers, clients or industry experts that endorse your brand.

8. Contact Information:

Clear details on how the media can reach your PR contact or you.

9. Social Media Links

10. Video Content (Optional):

Any relevant video content, such as promotional videos, interviews or event footage.

APPENDIX D:
LIST OF PR TOOLS AND RESOURCES

Here are a few free resources and tools that can help you search for and monitor PR opportunities:

1. Journalist requests:

X (Formerly Twitter): Search #journorequest to discover daily opportunities to secure press coverage

SourceBottle: A global publicity platform where you can gain access to press opportunities direct to your inbox

Connectively: Used to be called Help A Reporter or Haro. Sign up for access to international media opportunities.

In the Spotlight: PR membership with access to hundreds of UK media opportunities each week.

2. Media Monitoring:

Google Alerts: Free tool for monitoring your brand mentions across the web.

3. Press Release Distribution:

PR Sync/News by Wire: Free press release distribution services

4. Influencer Databases:

HypeAuditor/Collabstr: Free platforms for finding and collaborating with influencers in your niche.

5. PR Analytics Tool:

Google Analytics: Tracks the effectiveness of PR campaigns by analysing website traffic and user behaviour.

6. Networking and Event Platforms:

LinkedIn: Invaluable for professional networking, establishing thought leadership and finding media contacts.

Eventbrite: Helps you manage and promote events as well as attend them.

Meetup: Great for organising and attending industry-related networking events.

APPENDIX E: CASE STUDY SUMMARIES

Below you'll find summaries of the case studies mentioned in the book where celebs leveraged their fame for social impact, highlighting what worked, what didn't and why.

1. Kim Kardashian and Criminal Justice Reform:

- **What Worked:** Kim Kardashian used her large social media following and high-profile connections to shine a spotlight on criminal justice reform. Her influence led to the early release of Alice Marie Johnson, showing how celebrity clout can push real change.
- **What Didn't:** Some people felt that Kim's involvement took the spotlight away from long-time activists and the broader movement.
- **Key Takeaway:** Celebrities can bring much-needed attention to important causes, but it's important to make sure the focus stays on the issue, not just the famous face behind it.

2. Marcus Rashford and Child Food Security:

- **What Worked:** Rashford's personal story about growing up with food insecurity made his campaign to tackle child hunger feel genuine and heartfelt. As a Premier League star, his voice carried weight and led to a major policy change in the UK.

- **What Didn't:** There was some political pushback, but Rashford's consistent, authentic messaging won out in the end.
- **Key Takeaway:** When you have a personal connection to the cause, it gives your PR campaign more power and credibility, especially when tackling big social issues.

3. Celeste Barber and Australian Bushfire Relief:

- **What Worked:** Celeste Barber used her down-to-earth humour and huge social media presence to raise over $51 million for bushfire relief. Her relatable style helped the campaign go viral.
- **What Didn't:** There were some legal hurdles about how the funds could be distributed, which shows that you need a solid plan and clear communication when running charitable campaigns.
- **Key Takeaway:** Going viral can be a game-changer, but it's crucial to have all the details sorted out in advance to avoid complications later.

These examples show how the right PR campaign, powered by celebrity influence, can be leveraged to create meaningful change but also highlight the importance of effective planning and keeping the focus on the matter at hand.

APPENDIX F: PRESS RELEASE TEMPLATES

Though not essential to securing coverage, press releases are a great way to distribute key information about your business. Here's a couple of successful releases created for clients for past clients with notes to help you craft your own.

YOUR LOGO

For Immediate release or
Release Date/Embargoed until: (An embargo will usually no more than a week ahead and should coincide with the launch of the biz, product or service. Only used if essential that the story is not released earlier and to make sure one outlet doesn't release the story to far in advance of others)

Business Set Up By Best Friends Goes Viral After Taking Advice From Richard Branson

(Headline should sum up and explain the angle of the story. Catchy headline - Needs to grab the reader –Think Daily Mail Who, what, when, why, where and why should the READER care?)

www.mylockerworld.co.uk
Good place to put your email address

First paragraph(s) should sum up the angle of the story. Think of your story as an upside down pyramid. All of the juicy, most exciting information should be at the top. This paragraph is your only opportunity to maintain the interest of the journalist. It should act as a summary or precursor to the meat of the story. Danielle Bloggs and Lara Bloggs, two best friends and mumpreneurs from London, have found themselves going viral after taking Richard Branson's advice to 'put themselves on the frontline' of their business.

Danielle posted a video on her personal Facebook profile of her demonstrating how easy it is to decorate the bespoke lockers she supplies for teens. She had hoped that a few friends would share the video but was blown away when it hit over 18,000 views and 170 shares in just 24 hours. Thanks to the power of social media word has spread up and down the country and has had over 24,000 views.

The following paragraph(s) should explain how the business or service began/what inspired the launch? You should also include any notable information/accolades/awards/celebrity ambassadors etc

Further information should include key background information on the service or product. What is it made from? Where is it available? Why is it different to competitor's products? What's the cost?

Danielle and Lara started the business in July 2016 with the help of Startup Loan. Despite having seven children between them the best friends didn't let this deter them from pursuing their entrepreneurial dream.

The idea came about after Danielle's daughter Leah, who was eleven at the time, decided she wanted a locker for her room that she could decorate like they do in the American TV series'. When Danielle realised nothing like this was available she bought an industrial locker, which she decorated herself. Leah was so happy with the finished product she persuaded her mum to set up a business making the lockers. The business is already making a profit having sold 150 of the lockers so far.

Having always worked in retail, this is the first business set up the ladies. Further to their

Following paragraphs must include key background information on the service or product. What is it made from? Where is it available? Why is it different to competitor's products? What's the cost? With such vast experience under his belt it would be easy to believe that Carr had been designing for far longer than a decade. It appears that creativity runs in the family. Carr credits his mother who worked as a seamstress for helping him discover his talent. Receiving his first sewing machine at 18, Carr stayed up for two days making his first garment. From that day he knew it was what he wanted to do for a living.

Described by Carr as "having more engineering than a smart phone", EVC garments are carefully and technically engineered to a high specification, combining high-quality fabric, vibrancy and innovative design. The occasion wear collection, created to instill confidence in the wearer, delivers a selection of striking but feminine pieces, which redefine power dressing and off-duty chic. The ability to deliver haute couture styling at an accessible price will undoubtedly help cement EVCs position as an exclusive heritage British fashion brand.

The collection is available from EVC's online store. Prices start at £181.

(Final paragraph must include contact information)

-ENDS-

For further information contact: .....

Insert phone number (office) – indicate any timings re availability – Mon to Fri, 9am to 5pm

Insert mobile number and availability

Insert email address

Notes to Editors:

1. The full collection is available through the website www.emilevidalcarr.com

2. Points under notes to editors would be numbered

Include, in notes to editors, standard information which explains what your organisation does. This is also known as your boilerplate. Here is an example of my previous boilerplate:

About Brenda Gabriel PR

Biz Game changer Public Relations (BGPR) was founded in 2014 by former civil service project and communications manager, Brenda Gabriel.

Having spent time working with one of London's most high profile PR agencies (with client rosters which included globally renowned names such as Sir Bob Geldof, Samuel L Jackson and Kellie Rowland), Brenda has learnt her craft from one of the industry's best.

Armed with national and international relationships and a passion for effecting positive change. Brenda set up Biz Gamechanger to on the representation of disruptors, change makers and innovators.

EMILE VIDAL CARR

For immediate release or
Release Date/Embargoed until: (An embargo will usually no more than a week ahead and should coincide with the launch of the biz, product or service. Only used if essential that the story is not released earlier and to make sure one outlet doesn't release the story to far in advance of others)

London Designer brings structural 'engineering' to the fore of women's occasion wear with vivid futuristic collection
(Headline should sum up and explain the angle of the story. Catchy headline - Needs to grab the reader –Think Daily Mail Who, what, when, why, where and why should the READER care?)

www.emilevidalcarr.com -
Good place to put your email address

First paragraph should sum up the angle of the story. Think of your story as an upside down pyramid. All of the juicy, most exciting information should be at the top. This paragraph is your only opportunity to maintain the interest of the journalist. It should act as a summary or precursor to the meat of the story.
If you haven't yet heard of Emile Carr, that is set to change. Fresh from working on the Alexander McQueen collection for Paris Fashion Week, London's hottest new designer has launched his premium fashion label Emile Vidal Carr. 29-year-old Carr is no stranger to fashion success having previously designed a range for high street and online giants including Topshop and ASOS upon graduating from the prestigious London College of Fashion.

The second paragraph should explain how the business or service began/what inspired the launch? This paragraph should also include any notable information/accolades/awards/celebrity ambassadors etc
Launched in 2013 the Emile Vidal Carr collection was inspired by Carr's passion for architecture and the desire to create structured, wearable, fashion for women crafted from technical fabrics. Carr's first premium collection was constructed from soundproofing fabric.

"I love architecture' says founder Emile, so I use my fascination for structure and translate that into my designs, which adds to our very distinctive style."

The incredibly talented and accomplished Head Designer Carr, whose CV reads like a who's-who of 21st century fashion houses has worked on collections for Roland Mouret, Victoria Beckham, Erdem, Peter Pilotto and Kanye West. In 2008 Carr was one of 20 designers chosen to take part in New York Fashion Week. He was also part of the team responsible for producing the 2012 Australian Olympic team uniforms. Carr's designs have been spotted on the likes of presenter Tess Daly for an appearance on Strictly Come Dancing and MOBO awards founder, Kanya King, MBE.

APPENDIX G: FURTHER READING AND RESOURCES

For those looking to deepen their knowledge and continue learning about PR, fame, celebrity and becoming a catalyst for change, here are some recommended books, articles and online resources:

Books:

- *Spin Sucks: Communication and Reputation Management in the Digital Age* by Gini Dietrich
- *The Fame Formula* by Mark Borkowski
- *Purpose* by Jessica Huie
- *Fame 101* by Jay and Maggie Jessup
- *Building a Storybrand* by Donald Miller
- *Extremely Online* by Taylor Lorenz

Articles:

- 'The Evolution of PR in the Digital Age' - *PR Week*
- 'The PESO Model: What It Is and Why It Matters' - *Spin Sucks*
- 'Celebrity Activists: Stars Using Their Voices for Good - *US Weekly*

Online Resources:

- PRSA (Public Relations Society of America) – www.prsa.org
- CIPR (Chartered Institute of Public Relations) – www.cipr.co.uk
- Spin Sucks – www.spinsucks.com

APPENDIX H: CHOOSING A PR AGENCY

Selecting the right PR agency is crucial to ensuring you get the best experience and achieve your desired results. Remember, PR is about building relationships. The relationship you have with your agency is just as important as the one you will build with the media. Here are some considerations to ensure the right fit:

Experience: Does the agency have experience in your specific industry, or are they willing to dive in and learn quickly? Every industry has its nuances and the best PR campaigns reflect that. An agency with relevant experience will likely already have strategies, contacts and insights to achieve your goals. Even if they don't, they should express an interest to learn about the space you operate in.

Success Stories: Can they provide case studies or testimonials from past clients? Ask for specifics: What types of results have they delivered in the past? Have they successfully navigated challenges similar to yours? Sometimes these success stories won't be advertised on their website, as clients often request confidentiality, so don't be afraid to ask directly. A good agency will have examples at the ready or be able to speak in detail about past wins.

Alignment: Do the agency's values and approach align with your brand? PR is about storytelling, so it's important the agency understands and supports the story you want to tell. A mismatch can lead to campaigns that don't resonate with your audience—or worse, damage your brand's reputation. It's important that they "get" what you stand for.

Network: Do they have established media contacts and relationships within your industry? PR is about connections. While agencies don't have magical powers to guarantee coverage, strong relationships with the right journalists, influencers, and platforms can make a significant difference in securing valuable media attention. Ask about their media reach: What kind of connections do they have? Do they understand which outlets are most relevant for you?

Transparency: Are they clear about their process, pricing, and what you can realistically expect from their services? The world of PR can be a bit ambiguous, so you want an agency that's upfront about what they can deliver. Are they providing you with a clear breakdown of costs, or are they being vague? Can they explain what success looks like in measurable terms? Transparency will help you avoid frustrations down the line.

Strategy: Do they offer a strategic plan tailored to your goals? Look for more than just enthusiasm. Ask if they've thought critically about what you need and how they'll get you there. Are they just talking about tactics (e.g., media coverage), or are they bringing a broader, long-term vision to the table? An agency should be able to outline a PR plan that is as much about strategy as it is about execution.

Communication: Are they responsive and easy to communicate with? PR often requires quick turnarounds and on-the-fly adjustments, so you'll want to work with a team that's responsive, proactive, and transparent in their communication. If it's difficult to get clear answers in the early stages, that's a red flag. Great PR agencies act as true partners, staying in constant touch to keep you informed and on the same page.

Cultural Fit: Can you see yourself working closely with them over time? PR isn't a one-off transaction; it's a long-term relationship. You'll be spending significant time collaborating with this team, so ask yourself if you feel comfortable with them. Can you be candid with them about your needs? Are they people you feel you can trust to represent your brand effectively? If it feels forced or uncomfortable from the start, it may not be the right fit.

APPENDIX I:
SAMPLE PR BUDGET BREAKDOWN

Understanding where your money goes in a PR campaign can help you manage expectations and plan effectively. Here's a sample budget breakdown:

1. **Agency Fees**: 40% of budget. Typically covering the retainer or fees paid to the PR agency for their strategic planning, media outreach, and campaign management.
2. **Media Monitoring**: 5% of budget. This includes tools and software to track media mentions, coverage and public sentiment
3. **Content Creation**: 10% of budget. This covers creating press releases, articles, blogs, videos, social media content and other assets for the campaign.
4. **Events and Activations**: 15% of budget. If events, product launches, or activations are part of the strategy, this would include venue costs, logistics, promotions, and guest management.
5. **Influencer Partnerships**: 10% of budget. This includes fees paid to influencers, content collaborations, and campaign promotions.
6. **Advertising and Paid Media**: 10% of budget. Covers paid ads on traditional and digital platforms to amplify reach, such as social media ads, Google Ads or paid sponsorships.
7. **Miscellaneous**: 5-10% of budget. Includes any unplanned expenses such as travel, last-minute opportunities, or unforeseen costs during the campaign.

Some agencies, such as mine, will include much of the above as part of their service. Remember to ask what's included in the retainer and expect to pay more based on how much of the costs above they absorb.

This sample breakdown will vary depending on the agency you choose and the needs of your campaign, but it's a good starting point for understanding the costs involved.

CONCLUSION

The appendices are designed to be your go-to reference to help you understand the strategies and insights from this book. PR can be a maze, but with the right tools, knowledge and support, you can navigate it successfully and achieve your goals. Whether you're growing your personal brand, launching a new product or positioning your business as an industry leader, these resources will help you on your journey.

ACKNOWLEDGMENTS

For Brad, who always reminds me how capable I am.

For K-Ci, Joshua, and Amelia-Sophia, who make every step of the journey worthwhile and inspire me to be the best version of myself.

To Katie, my incredible EA, for keeping her foot on my neck through the entire process and making sure this book happened.

To Kat, my tech whiz friend, whose amazing advice helped me bite the bullet and get this book started.

To Tina, for always reminding me to remember who the f£ck I am.

To my sister Scarlet, who kept reminding me how important this book would be.

To Rebecka, who helped crystallise my vision for the future of PR.

And to every client who trusted me to elevate their PR and every follower who gives me a reason to show up and share my thoughts daily—this book is for you.

AUTHOR BIO

Brenda Gabriel is a publicist and personal branding expert with over 15 years' experience in the field. Specialising in helping entrepreneurs, executives and influencers, build high-impact personal brands, Brenda has worked with notable figures such as Taban Shoresh, a genocide survivor and founder of the Lotus Flower charity, as well as the late Richard Taylor OBE and the Damilola Taylor Trust.

Known for her expertise in both traditional PR and the digital landscape, Brenda has consistently delivered results for her clients by securing top-tier media placements, building impactful personal brands, and creating celebrity connections that elevate visibility and influence. She is also a regular media commentator on PR and celebrity personal branding, sharing her insights on how to navigate the ever-evolving world of publicity.

Brenda blends traditional media and strategies with metaphysical insights and a focus on emotional resilience, ensuring clients are not only visible but fully prepared for increased fame, fortune and demands of life in the public eye.

www.facebook.com/brenda.gabriel

www.linkedin.com/in/brendagabriel/

www.brendagabriel.co.uk

Printed in Great Britain
by Amazon

53668918R00142